He Made Ice and Changed the World

THE STORY OF FLORIDA'S
John Gorrie

Linda Hansen Caldwell
Cover Illustrator: Karen Atkins

HE MADE ICE AND CHANGED THE WORLD: THE STORY OF FLORIDA'S JOHN GORRIE

1405 SW 6th Avenue • Ocala, Florida 34471 • Phone 352-622-1825 • Fax 352-622-1875
Website: www.atlantic-pub.com • Email: sales@atlantic-pub.com
SAN Number: 268-1250

Library of Congress Cataloging-in-Publication Data

Names: Caldwell, Linda Hansen, 1954- author.
Title: He made ice and changed the world : the story of John Gorrie / by Linda Hansen Caldwell.
Description: Ocala : Atlantic Publishing Group, Inc., [2019] | Includes bibliographical references and index. | Summary: "This is the story of one of America's most respected humanitarians, Dr. John Gorrie (1803-1855). He was a physician, inventor, scientist, elected official, and a public health educator—a true Florida hero! Dr. Gorrie's interest in tropical diseases, specifically yellow fever and malaria, led him to Apalachicola, Florida. There, he practiced medicine in his office and two hospitals, and was nicknamed "The Fever Man." A man of tue compassion, Dr. Gorrie even used the second floor of his home to treat sick patients. Tropical diseases shaped the history of the South, where yearly epidemics claimed thousands of lives. The desire to comfort patients led to his inventions, and we can thank Dr. Gorrie for refrigeration, air conditioning, and ice! Today, every machine that cools the air relies on John Gorrie's research and principles! Dr. Gorrie's original ice machine is housed in the Smithsonian Museum, and he is a member of the Florida Inventor's Hall of Fame. After reading Dr. Gorrie's biography, you may want to visit Florida's Panhandle, where you will find the Gorrie Bridge and the John Gorrie State Park & Museum"—Provided by publisher.
Identifiers: LCCN 2019046649 | ISBN 9781620236925 (paperback) | ISBN 9781620236932 (ebook)
Subjects: LCSH: Gorrie, John, 1803-1855—Health. | Physicians—Florida—Apalachicola—Biography. | Inventors—Florida—Apalachicola—Biography. | Refrigeration and refrigerating machinery—United States—History.
Classification: LCC R154.G67 C35 2019 | DDC 610.92 [B]—dc23
LC record available at https://lccn.loc.gov/2019046649

Printed in the United States

PROJECT MANAGER: Meaghan Summers
INTERIOR LAYOUT AND JACKET DESIGN: Nicole Sturk

Over the years, we have adopted a number of dogs from rescues and shelters. First there was Bear and after he passed, Ginger and Scout. Now, we have Kira, another rescue. They have brought immense joy and love not just into our lives, but into the lives of all who met them.

We want you to know a portion of the profits of this book will be donated in Bear, Ginger and Scout's memory to local animal shelters, parks, conservation organizations, and other individuals and nonprofit organizations in need of assistance.

– Douglas & Sherri Brown,
President & Vice-President of Atlantic Publishing

T HIS IS ALMOST certainly a motto that Dr. Gorrie would ascribe to if he were alive today. I had it posted on the wall in my high school classroom.

"There are always those that will attempt to discourage you as you work to achieve an admirable goal. When that happens, make another goal, that being to ignore them."

—Linda Hansen Caldwell

Dedication

THIS BOOK IS dedicated to the descendants of Dr. John Gorrie, the students of John Gorrie Elementary School, and the alumni of John Gorrie Jr. High School. It is further dedicated to Linda's grandchildren (Morgan, Gloria, Killian, and Brice), and to Karen's daughter, Katelyn.

Table of Contents

Foreword

Robert Watson, MD
Professor, Florida State University College of Medicine

JOHN GORRIE, MD, was a truly remarkable individual. He practiced medicine for only 18 years, but, during those years, he accomplished more in both the art and science of medicine than physicians who practiced for decades longer. He provided care to his patients and cared about them, their families, and his community. Dr. Gorrie utilized the most up-to-date treatments available during the mid-19th century and also recognized that prevention of illness was more important than the cure, as many more lives could be saved through prevention rather than treatment. His tireless efforts were not driven by fame and fortune, but by compassion and dedication for feverish patients, a desire to prevent illness, and a concern for community health. He was a true humanitarian and keeper of the Hippocratic Oath (i.e., the oath physicians historically took).

While practicing medicine in Apalachicola, Florida, a small rural town located in the panhandle of Florida, he exemplified a physician's obligation to the health and welfare of the community, not merely that of individual patients. John Gorrie focused on public health, setting a precedent by becoming a public health physician and educator.

It is difficult to imagine that this young man, whose only knowledge of physics was from a book he read during medical school, was able to conceive of and build a machine that would change the course of history. His interest in thermodynamics helped him invent the first machine that could compress air; upon controlled release of that compressed air, the temperature of that air would be lowered sufficiently to make artificial ice. Dr. Gorrie's work was sometimes ridiculed more than revered. In the decades following his death, his contributions received little of the acknowledgment they deserved. In hindsight, it is remarkable that Dr. Gorrie didn't receive a Nobel Prize or its equivalent and that he didn't amass a fortune.

Dr. Gorrie was a quiet and humble man who was not capable of being a salesman—whether for his ice machine or himself. His lack of fame and fortune was not of concern to him. It is reasonable to assume that Dr. Gorrie recognized that his goal of saving countless lives had not come to fruition; this overwhelmed his spirit and weakened him, likely leading to his untimely death. There was no way he could have known that, following his death, his ice machine would lead to what he envisioned and far more. The endless inventions that ultimately came from his creation of the first air compressor that cooled the air have aided in the prevention of some diseases, the effective treatment of many others, and the comfort of untold millions of people and other creatures.

Dr. Gorrie had many characteristics that should be emulated—not only by physicians but also by everyone. He was unpretentious, worked hard, saw problems, and tried to solve them. His was a life of service to others. It can be hoped that his legacy will be even further recognized, and this biography will be vital to that outcome. We should join the students of John Gorrie Elementary School in Tampa, Florida, who respect and admire Dr. Gorrie as an outstanding American and strive to preserve his legacy.

Robert Watson, MD, is a 1969 graduate of the University of Florida College of Medicine (UF COM), where he was elected to the Alpha Omega Alpha Honor Society. He served as a Professor of Neurology, Neuroscience, and Clinical Neurology at the University of Florida for more than three decades. He also served as the Senior Associate Dean for Educational Affairs at the University of Florida College of Medicine for 17 years and as the Jules B. Chapman, MD Professor of Clinical Care and Humaneness for 12 years. Dr. Watson served as the Vice Chair of the Department of Neurology. As

Senior Associate Dean for Educational Affairs, Dr. Watson was delegated authority for undergraduate medical, physician assistant, graduate biomedical, graduate medical, and continuing medical education. From 2009–2013, he served as the Executive Associate Dean for Administrative Affairs at Florida State University College of Medicine (FSU COM). He is currently a professor of neurology at FSU COM and professor emeritus of the UF COM.

Dr. Watson was Chair of the Association of American Medical College (AAMC)'s Group on Educational Affairs in 2001, and he has served on several AAMC committees. He is an acknowledged authority on curriculum and is recognized as an outstanding teacher, student advocate, and leader in his profession. He received the Hippocratic Award from the UF COM Class of 1985, the highest honor that can be bestowed upon a faculty member. Dr. Watson has served on state, regional, and national committees that involve medical education, funding for the continuation of medical education and physician workforce. He currently serves on the Executive Committee of Florida's Professional Resource Network Board of Directors. Dr. Watson is a Trustee of the Jules B. Chapman and Annie Lou Chapman Private Foundation, where he endeavors to fulfill Dr. and Mrs. Chapman's goal to improve humanism in medicine and medical education.

Introduction

D R. GORRIE'S LEGACY has been debated for years since his passing in 1855. After all, there were so many other inventors in the world; why would anyone focus on a quiet man from Florida? Despite Dr. Gorrie's achievements, very few knew of him. This fact also became clear to the U.S. architect of the Capitol in 1910 as he walked through Washington, D.C. A noted Congressman from New York City boarded the train he was on and pleasantly fell into conversation with the architect. After exchanging some pleasantries, the architect stated that he hailed from "the land of flowers"—Florida. The Congressman stated, "You have had no great men in that state." Without a statue in the Hall of Fame in Washington and both of the state's places being vacant, the architect couldn't convince the Congressman otherwise. However, he soon assured him that Florida had "many men worthy of this honor" and that, "'ere another session of the Florida Legislature closed," there would be a statue in the Hall of Fame representing Florida. With that, Dr. Gorrie's statue was underway.

In the fall of 1980, I was beginning my fifth year of teaching. I graduated from the University of Florida in 1976, and, in early 1977, I began teaching in the public schools. I was proud to work for the Duval County Public School system because I had attended Jacksonville public schools from K–12.

I had been transferred three times as a result of court-ordered racial balancing. I waited by the telephone (there were no cell phones in 1980), expecting to learn where I would be assigned if I were re-hired. I was certified to teach in several subject areas, so my chance of being re-hired was better than it was for others. I received a call from Human Resources, telling me that John Gorrie Jr. High School had an opening, and I was to report to the Principal that morning. I didn't know it at the time, but this would be the start of something significant in my life.

I drove to the campus, knowing that school would be starting in a couple of days. The first thing I noticed as I approached the campus was that *all* of the windows were open; the school was not air-conditioned. I wasn't pleased about that, but I knew I could make the best of the situation. I walked into the main building and asked where I could find the Principal, Dr. Jerry Gugel. When I knocked on his door, Dr. Gugel greeted me and shook my hand. I told him my name was Linda Hansen. *"Miss Hansen,"* he said, *"you're the new health and science teacher, right?"* I replied, *"That's me."* He said, *"I'm on my way to a faculty meeting. Follow me."*

Once we arrived at the faculty meeting in the air-conditioned Media Center, Dr. Gugel began introducing new faculty members. I met the other teachers in my department. As the meeting ended, the Media Specialist, Mrs. Jean Powell, and her assistant, Mrs. Olwen Webb, showed me around and said they would be *"happy to assist me with anything I needed."* Their kindness made me feel very welcome.

There was much for me to do. I would be teaching subjects I had not taught previously. I began to settle into room 204 in the main building. There were textbooks and other items to inventory, and I was pleased to learn that the previous teacher had left copies of items that would prove valuable. I was probably the last teacher to leave campus that day. After a long day spent working in a hot classroom, I headed home. I was looking forward to a new school year, and I knew I would make the best of it.

As I was going through my teaching materials that evening, reading the textbooks and making lesson plans, I began to wonder ... *who is John Gorrie?* I knew he must be someone special or he wouldn't have a school named after him. I was determined to learn about the man.

After the first few days of school, I had a chance to catch my breath. I visited the Media Center during my planning period and took a few encyclopedias off the shelf (there was no internet in 1980). As I began to read about Dr. Gorrie, I was quite impressed with his accomplishments; he was a pioneer in the field of refrigeration and air conditioning. *How ironic*, I thought, *John Gorrie Jr. High School isn't air-conditioned.* It seemed like *this* school would be first on the list when it came to air conditioning.

On a positive note, however, I knew this teaching assignment would provide me with an exciting opportunity. Not only would I be teaching science and health, I could also relate Dr. Gorrie's accomplishments to my lessons! I could teach my students about the school's namesake as I followed my course objectives.

In 1982, I learned that Dr. Gorrie's first biography was in our Media Center. I was one of the first people to check out *The Fever Man.* As I read it, I learned that not only was Dr. Gorrie a physician, scientist, and inventor, but he was also a public health educator! As the years passed, I became one of Dr. Gorrie's "cheerleaders." Whenever I had an opportunity to tell someone about Dr. Gorrie, I did.

I had been teaching at John Gorrie Jr. High School for several years when I met and fell in love with Gregory Caldwell, and we became engaged in 1983. We married shortly after that, and I gave birth to our daughter, Brittany Lin, in 1985.

In the fall of 1987, Frito-Lay transferred my husband to Orlando. I began the next school year at Gateway High School in Kissimmee, teaching Biology and Anatomy & Physiology. As my career progressed through the years, I taught many other students in other settings. Of course, I never forgot about Dr. Gorrie; whenever his accomplishments coincided with the course objectives, I mentioned him.

Fast forward to 2017: a student came to me, asking for assistance. He needed to check out a biography of a famous scientist or inventor for a book report. He asked if I have any suggestions. Of course, the first person I thought of was Dr. Gorrie. *The Fever Man* was not available. I learned it was no longer in print; no one had published a biography on Dr. Gorrie since 1982! A librarian in my local public library said she would try to find a copy that I could borrow.

A few days later, my librarian found a copy of *The Fever Man*. I was saddened to learn, however, that the only one she could find was in Alabama! Students in Florida couldn't check out a book about Dr. Gorrie. As one of our nation's most respected and most accomplished individuals, and, as a Floridian, John Gorrie's book should be availble in every school library in Florida.

I spoke to officials at the Gorrie State Park Museum and learned the museum staff had been seeking for a person who would be willing to write a new biography for quite some time. I spoke to a Dean at the UF College of Medicine and also discussed the situation with the acquisitions librarian in my county library system. I was encouraged to write a new biography, and I was told, *"You are the perfect person to write it! Please do! If you don't write it, who will?"*

There were so many "stories" about Dr. Gorrie already written, but many were misleading or simply inaccurate. Because Dr. Gorrie's records (personal, patient, and research) had been accidentally destroyed, we do not know much about him. Still, I knew I needed to write about John Gorrie's life. I had done some professional writing in the past; I felt I could combine my writing experience with my admiration for Dr. Gorrie. Being retired, I had time to devote to the project. I decided I would write a new biography on Dr. Gorrie.

While it does not describe all the details of his life, this biography tells of Dr. Gorrie's tremendous concern for his fellow man, great struggle, sacrifice, and accomplishments. Although this story ends sadly for John Gorrie, this biography is a remembrance of his dedicated and conscientious work.

Dr. Gorrie deserved a new biography more than anyone I knew. Some individuals stand out as truly compassionate humanitarians. Dr. John Gorrie (1803–55) was one such person. As a young man, perhaps in part due to the way he was raised, he developed an interest in helping mankind, and this interest remained with him throughout his life. His interests and talents enabled him to become a scientist, an inventor, a public servant, and a health educator. But, most of all, Dr. Gorrie was a physician, and he took that responsibility very seriously. Although the practice of medicine in the 1800s was crude as compared to today, he was determined to be the best physician possible and certainly strove to provide the very best medical treatment under circumstances that were not enviable. He earned the deep respect of his fellow colleagues. Very few compare to Dr. Gorrie and the high professional and personal standards he placed upon himself.

Dr. Gorrie was a quiet, reserved, and humble person who was driven to comfort patients, and perhaps, cure them of malaria and yellow fever. These devastating tropical diseases recurred year after year when the weather turned warm. Tropical disease epidemics literally shaped the history of the South, especially Florida. During these epidemics, Dr. Gorrie would often work himself to exhaustion. One can only imagine how helpless he sometimes felt as he treated patients against seemingly impossible odds. The survival rates for malaria and yellow fever were quite low and, as each epidemic came along, he hoped to learn more about the causes and the best treatments for each disease.

Although Dr. Gorrie was the community physician and a resident at two hospitals, he was a deep thinker, and simply working as a physician did not satisfy him. When Gorrie observed community health problems, such as sanitation issues, he set about to solve these problems by using the scientific method. Further, he understood that public education could go a long way toward improving public health. After being appointed to his first position of public office, city councilman, he recognized an opportunity—a platform that allowed him to influence the health of the public at large. He urged other public officials to address public health issues, as well. He was later elected Mayor, allowing him to further educate the public and improve the health of his community. This aspect of his life is less mentioned, but it set him aside from other public officials of his day. He was one of the first of his day to address poor "lifestyle" as it relates to health. This was no easy task during a time when belief in "old wives' tales" and superstition was common.

As a physician, Dr. Gorrie was determined to alleviate the intense suffering caused by the symptoms of yellow fever and malaria. He hypothesized that cooling the air would provide comfort and, perhaps, lead to an increased survival rate for his yellow fever and malaria patients. Developing a way to cool air would become a primary goal. The second part of his hypothesis proved to be wrong; cooling the air did not increase the survival rate, but Dr. Gorrie was certainly not a failure. He eventually gave up the practice of medicine, believing that he could save millions of lives through his refrigeration projects. Some would say he was compulsive about his work, spending extended periods without speaking to anyone else, completely absorbed in his efforts. Gorrie's research led to the invention of a specialized air compressor, a device that rapidly compresses and expands air to lower its temperature. The air compressor was the critical component of Dr. Gorrie's ice machine, and this machine became the precursor to all modern air conditioning and refrigeration machines, for they all utilize compressors as the key functioning unit.

Dr. Gorrie is recognized as "the father of refrigeration and air conditioning." Being first and foremost a physician, the commercial aspect and financial reward of air cooling, ice-making, and refrigeration was merely an afterthought. His inventions are far-reaching and have brought substantial benefit to everyone who lives today. Few would consider living without them. The availability of ice, no matter the season or location, helped to transform Florida and the nation as a whole. When there is an extended power outage, people quickly become concerned about the lack of refrigeration and ice. If the weather is warm, they miss the comfort provided by air conditioning. We enjoy a wide variety of foods as a result of refrigerated transportation. Tourism is an extremely important statewide industry that supports Florida's economy, and few would want to visit the Sunshine State without the comforts provided by Dr. Gorrie's inventions.

In addition to making us more comfortable during the warm months of the year, air conditioning significantly decreases humidity, or the amount of moisture in the air. High humidity is a key factor in the growth of molds, mildew, and bacteria. If allowed to grow, these organisms can cause infection, destroy homes, furnishings, clothes, and shoes. Today's businesses rely on air conditioning to maintain the quality of their inventory. Healthcare facilities rely on air conditioning to reduce the growth of bacteria and other microbes by keeping the air dry and cool as well as keeping patients and employees safe, comfortable, and productive. Many prescription medications must be refrigerated to maintain potency and quality. Computers, electronic servers, and other equipment function best when they are maintained at the proper temperature.

Despite his outstanding achievements, Dr. Gorrie was penniless at the time of his death. He and his relatives never received any financial compensation despite his U.S. patents. It has been said that Dr. Gorrie's work was "ahead of its time," for, if he had been born a few decades later, he would have likely enjoyed great satisfaction and pride—and a return on his investment. When you think of the time, money, energy, and dedication Gorrie put into his work, it is understandable that he died broken-hearted and humiliated because others simply couldn't see what he, himself, could see. Further, he was unsure about whom he could trust and was "stabbed in the back" by the "Ice Kings" in the North that harvested ice from frozen rivers and lakes; they knew they would lose a profitable business if Dr. Gorrie found success with his inventions. The media was unfair to him, too. Lack of success in the business aspect of his work was, undoubtedly, a tremendous source of frustration for John Gorrie, and he couldn't seem to get past it.

For a period of 51 years after Dr. Gorrie died, interest in the ice machine, refrigeration, and air conditioning faded into obscurity. Then, in the early 1900s, another inventor, Willis Carrier, somehow learned about Dr. Gorrie's patent information for mechanical air cooling. According to those familiar with the story, Carrier utilized Dr. Gorrie's principles in the manufacture of the first commercial air conditioners, for the Westinghouse Electric Company. Later, Carrier founded his own company, Carrier Air Conditioning, now called The Carrier Corporation. The Carrier Corporation proudly asserts that the company's founder, Willis Carrier, invented modern air conditioning and provides Dr. Gorrie no credit for his pioneering work. The Smithsonian Institute credits Dr. Gorrie alone with the invention of mechanical air cooling by use of an air compressor and his inventions were what led to the modern machines that keep us comfortable today. (The Smithsonian houses two types of items related to Willis Carrier—photographs and the Carrier Centrifugal Refrigeration Compressor, made in 1922, 67 years after Dr. Gorrie died.) Students studying to become HVAC (heating, ventilation, and air conditioning) technicians learn of Dr. Gorrie's principles and understand these principles to be the foundation of the very profitable HVAC industry.

It is quite likely that no one will ever know, with certainty, all of the facts concerning Dr. Gorrie's life, his dreams, and his important work. Over an extended period, various authors have written articles about this famous Floridian, but the dates of his various life events have been reported differently. Therefore, I have used the most-frequently reported dates and facts in this book. Although Gorrie's patent information and original ice machine are housed in the Smithsonian Institute, Dr. Gorrie's personal and patient records were lost. These records would likely tell of Dr. Gorrie's private thoughts—his concerns, his profession, and his optimism about what he hoped to accomplish during his life. The last biography of Dr. Gorrie, *The Fever Man*, authored by Vivian M. Sherlock, was published in 1982.

The interest in this biography has amazed me! As I traveled to take photographs and learn more about Dr. Gorrie, I met only one person who said discouraging words. As we were walking, I was trying to make pleasant conversation. It appeared to me that this individual had no respect for my goal or for Dr. Gorrie's commendable contributions to the way we live today. I did not allow this one person to crush my determination, however. This person was expressing the same negativity that Dr. Gorrie encountered as he pursued his work. He was ridiculed and discouraged, but, unlike me who faced only one negative person, Dr. Gorrie had many who put obstacles in his way. I am delighted that this project "landed in my lap." It is my hope this biography will help to preserve Dr. Gorrie's legacy for many years to come.

In June of 2019, I stood over Dr. Gorrie's grave and, with tears in my eyes, I said, *"I hope this biography makes you proud, Dr. Gorrie. I did my best."* Somehow, I think he may have heard me. As I walked away, I added, *"I think you'd like it!"*

---- CHAPTER 1 ----

A School gets Cool!

I MAGINE THIS: it's late May, 1987. You are in the seventh grade—your first year as a student at John Gorrie Jr. High, in Jacksonville, Florida. The address: 2525 College Street, Jacksonville, Florida, 32204. It's an old but beautiful school, having been built in 1923 and opened in 1924. The architecture complements other buildings in the Riverside community, and the St. Johns River, one of the few rivers in the world that flows north, is just a couple of miles away. The "Blue Devils" of John Gorrie Jr. High had great pride and tremendous school spirit. As a part of the Duval County Public School District, John Gorrie Jr. High was a great school, offering so much to students and the community. In the 1980s, the school was named a "National Model School." There was one big problem, however. The school was not air-conditioned. Every public school in Duval County was air-conditioned except John Gorrie Jr. High.

Earlier that school year, in September, parents came to campus to take part in the annual "Open House," an opportunity to meet teachers and administrators and "follow" their child's schedule, to learn a little bit about their day. Many parents who came to this year's Open House stayed only a few minutes, just long enough to hear the principal speak in the school auditorium. It was after 7 p.m., yet the temperature inside the school was well over 80°F. Caring, interested parents left early because it was so hot in the main school building; they were quite miserable.

The school year progressed after the Open House, and, on this day, everyone in your class is trying to pay attention to your teacher's health education lesson. Warm air rises, and your classroom is on the second floor, room 204. There is no thermometer on the wall but everyone knows it's hot, very uncomfortable, being midday. Although all the windows are open, the temperature is about 88°F. Whenever a welcome breeze passes through the window, the U.S. flag waves a little, and any unsecured papers take flight. Each school year, the school administrators held a "drawing" for any teachers that had no fan in their classroom, awarding about five large fans per year, but Mrs. Caldwell had never won that lottery. There was no fan in your classroom.

When you raise your hand to respond to your teacher's question, your notebook paper sticks to your arm. Sweat is running down the faces of the students, and clothes are wet with perspiration. Some of the girls in the class have started using folded pieces of paper to fan themselves. There are colorful bulletin boards but no posters or pictures on the wall, because tape won't stick to walls when the air is so humid. Even the death row inmates in Florida State Prison, in Starke, have air conditioning in their cells, but this school has none—that is, unless you visit the Music Building, the Media Center, or the administrative offices.

This week, your class is learning about communicable, or contagious, diseases. Your teacher has covered polio, smallpox, chicken pox, measles, diphtheria, tetanus, ringworm, and whooping cough, among others. Now, it's time to learn about tropical diseases such as dengue fever, yellow fever, and malaria. Mrs. Caldwell begins her lesson by talking about the man your school was named after—John Gorrie, MD.

"Dr. Gorrie is considered to be the father of air conditioning and refrigeration," she says. "His primary interest in medicine was tropical diseases, particularly malaria and yellow fever. He was a compassionate and dedicated physician who practiced medicine in Apalachicola, Florida, in the mid-1800s. He was born in 1803 and died in 1855, 164 years ago. When this school was built, Dr. Gorrie had been dead for 68 years."

Mrs. Caldwell points to a simple map of Florida she's drawn on the board, showing her students where Apalachicola is and explaining its relationship to the Gulf of Mexico, Jacksonville, and the state as a whole. Using a globe, she points out the equator and further explains that Florida, being close to the equator, is considered to be tropical. Mrs. Caldwell explained, "Tropical areas have warmer air and water than the rest of the world, and tropical diseases only infect those who live in these areas.

"Dr. Gorrie was a resident physician at two area hospitals, one being a military hospital, and served as an elected official. He also held several prestigious positions in his community such as postmaster, city councilman, and even mayor. Plus. he was an advocate for improving public health. There were no health teachers in the schools, like me, way back then. Dr. Gorrie was their health education teacher.

"Many times, in the history of Florida and other southern states, yellow fever and malaria killed many thousands of people. During the summer of 1841, there was a terrible epidemic of yellow fever in Florida. Dr. Gorrie witnessed the devastating symptoms, especially the fevers, brought on by these diseases. This is why some people called him 'The Fever Man.'

"Yellow fever is called 'yellow fever' because the patient's skin and eyes become yellow when their liver fails. Malaria causes internal bleeding, sweats and chills, blood problems, and respiratory failure. Some survived these diseases, but many, many people died from them. People were terrified and did strange things, including wearing necklaces made of garlic and burning very smelly things like sulfur compounds, to prevent these illnesses. These things didn't actually prevent malaria and yellow fever because they didn't address the actual cause of the illnesses. People avoided others during these epidemics, too. You can only imagine how terrified people were. After each epidemic, Dr. Gorrie's spirit was empty. He wondered if, this year, he'd finally learned something of value, something that would help treat his patients during the next epidemic that was sure to come.

"John Gorrie soon observed that yellow fever and malaria were uncommon during the cooler months but became common during the warmer months, so he, and others, hypothesized that warm air—"bad air" coming from rotting vegetation in the swamps—was the greatest factor involved in causing these diseases, along with excessive moisture in the air and the high temperatures. He didn't know that, in actuality, a tiny insect called the mosquito was at the heart of the problem. Further, his crude microscope was unable to visualize the microorganisms responsible for these diseases. As a scientist, Dr. Gorrie believed that, one day, 'the cause will reveal itself to time and adequate means of investigation.'

"Dr. Gorrie felt the best way to fight these diseases and comfort his patients was to cool the air around them. To ease the suffering of his feverish patients, and perhaps cure them of these tropical diseases, Dr. Gorrie knew he needed ice, but ice was extremely difficult to come by in the South, and, even when it was available, it was exorbitantly expensive. Ice cost several dollars per pound; it was a true luxury! He concluded that he needed a way to develop ice artificially. People believed this whole idea was preposterous, but Dr. Gorrie utilized the scientific method to design and build the very first machine that made artificial ice.

"Dr. Gorrie's ice machine worked by compressing air, and then expanding it. He was the first to utilize an air compressor as the primary component of a machine that cooled air, much like the air compressors found in today's modern air cooling systems. When air is expanded, or becomes less dense, the temperature falls. Dr. Gorrie used this concept to freeze the water in a large tank. However, with his first ice machine, this process took eight hours! Dr. Gorrie, then, suspended containers of the ice he made in sick rooms above patient beds. He cared so much about his patients that he used the entire second floor of his home as a sick ward. Air cooled as it flowed over the ice and this was the very first air conditioning system!"

Photo credit: Florida State Archives

At this moment, a couple of the students giggle, and a few raise their hand to ask a very logical question: "Why, then, Mrs. Caldwell, if our school is named after the man who invented a way to cool air and make ice, don't *we* have air conditioning?"

John Gorrie Jr. High School had cold water fountains, and there was an ice machine in the cafeteria, but the school wasn't air conditioned because the voters in Duval County kept "voting it down." After all, these voters went to school without air conditioning, so they believed today's kids could do without it as well. Though, funding for air conditioning finally became available in 1986, and students, faculty, and staff learned that, one day in the future, cool air would come through those big green pipes that had been installed throughout the campus.

At just that moment, several workmen (air conditioning contractors) are heard speaking in the hallway. Their heavy boots make a distinctive sound as they walk through the halls. One sweaty workman enters your class-room, apologizes for the interruption, and walks toward an open window. He leans outside and yells "OK" to the workmen below. Everyone in your class is watching and thinking. *Maybe this will be the day that everyone has been waiting for. Dr. Gorrie would surely be happy if he could be here for this!*

The class is silent in anticipation of what would happen next. The huge green pipe in your classroom becomes the focus of attention. In a matter of minutes, cool air begins flowing through the pipe and many students rush to stand under it.

Mrs. Caldwell announces, "This is a huge day—an important moment in the history of this school!"

Some students in the class rise from their desks and begin closing the windows; after all, their homes are air conditioned, and they know windows should be closed.

The workman says, "This is only a brief test; it isn't going to last." He then walks to the window again, telling the workmen below to turn the units off. This was only a short test, but it certainly would have pleased Dr. Gorrie immensely.

Mrs. Caldwell asks the workman, "Do you know who the father of air conditioning is, the person who invented the first method of cooling the air by using an air compressor?"

The workman shrugs his shoulders, indicating that he didn't know the answer to that question. Enthusiastically, a few students point to the blackboard, where their teacher had written important facts about Dr. Gorrie. The workman doesn't seem very impressed, nevertheless, saying, "I never heard of him." He waves "goodbye" to the students, and, as he leaves the classroom, Mrs. Caldwell asks, "When will the testing be over?"

The workman says, "I don't know, Ma'am," and leaves the classroom.

Mrs. Caldwell resumes her lesson about tropical diseases, telling the students it would take a couple of days to discuss all of them. She places the most emphasis, however, on yellow fever and malaria—two diseases that were Dr. Gorrie's primary professional interest. "Dr. Gorrie's practice of medicine was unlike what you experience when you visit your doctor today. When you visit your doctor, they take your blood pressure with a machine called a sphygmomanometer. You are weighed on a scale. Your temperature is taken with a modern thermometer. Your ears are examined with an otoscope. You can only imagine how physicians in Dr. Gorrie's day struggled to determine what was wrong with a patient. Without modern medical equipment, a doctor had to rely on effective communication from the patient and anything he was able to observe during examination. The best doctors were those who had a great deal of experience from other physicians they studied under."

After answering a few questions from the students, it is time for class to be over. "We'll talk more about communicable diseases, tomorrow." Mrs. Caldwell assigns homework, and the students prepare to leave for their next class. This has been a memorable class session. Class ends with Mrs. Caldwell's comment: "Go home and tell your parents that we are finally getting air conditioning. It is really happening."

There is lots of chatter throughout the campus regarding the new air conditioning systems. Some of the teachers who were employed at the school for many years, or even for their entire career, have difficulty believing that air conditioning is finally going to be a part of their workday. There is much discussion and tremendous excitement throughout the buildings, especially at the lunch tables and in the faculty lounge—all thanks to Dr. Gorrie. *Wouldn't Dr. Gorrie be able to rest a little better, now, knowing a school named for him was finally going to be air-conditioned?*

In the school year 1987–1988, John Gorrie Jr. High School became fully air conditioned. It was reported that the air conditioning systems never worked very well, but at least the school, named after the "father of air conditioning and refrigeration" was finally air conditioned.

After the school closed in the summer of 1997, John Gorrie Jr. High School sat empty with a tall chain-link fence around it for nearly a decade. Unfortunately, there was some vandalism, and the beautiful architecture that was part of thousands of young lives became somewhat of an eyesore. A Jacksonville resident, Delores Barr Weaver, believed that the school should have a future. J. Wayne Weaver and his wife Delores, who, at the time, owned an

NFL football team—the Jacksonville Jaguars—purchased the abandoned school. Mrs. Weaver was very dedicated to preserving the campus, and over a long period of time, the campus was restored to its beauty. The completed project is a beautiful testament to the fact that dreams can come true. Individual residence units were built where classrooms once existed. John Gorrie Jr. High became The John Gorrie, a condominium complex. Each modern unit is, of course, air conditioned.

———— CHAPTER 2 ————

The Early Years

IF JOHN GORRIE were alive, now, in 2019, he would be celebrating his 216th birthday! Long ago, records of births and deaths were not widely recorded. In fact, no official government records were being kept. Generally, such records are only found in family Bibles. As new generations come along, there are conversations about family heritage, but memories fade and the spoken word is not always accurate. For this reason and others, there exists some confusion regarding John Gorrie's early life. Some of this confusion may relate to the fact that children born out of wedlock, as it is believed John Gorrie was, were sometimes shunned; they were referred to, quite negatively, as "bastards." There existed great shame in out-of-wedlock pregnancy.

It is believed John Gorrie was born on October 3, 1803 in the city of Charlestown, on the British island of Nevis in the West Indies. Nevis is a small island in the Caribbean Sea, east of Puerto Rico, far from the United States mainland. The map on the following page shows the islands of the region.

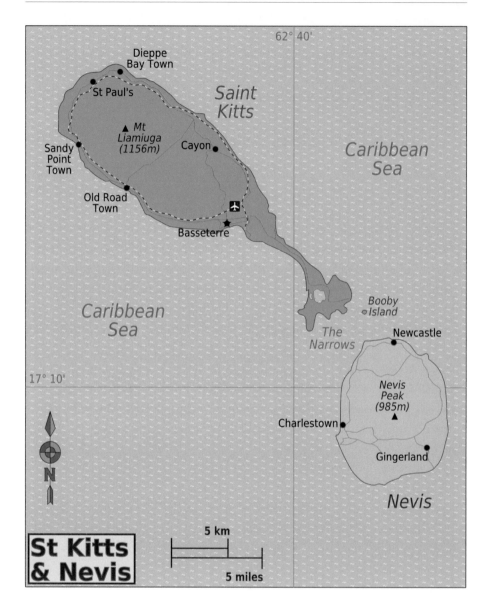

There is much vagueness concerning the circumstances of John Gorrie's birth. Some sources, including the memorial statue in Gorrie Square, cite Gorrie's date of birth in 1802, but more sources cite it in 1803. Dr. Gorrie's mother was unmarried, so there is no true knowledge of his father. During his adulthood, Dr. Gorrie appeared to have confided in a dear friend and colleague (Dr. Alvin W. Chapman), relating that he was not a "Gorrie" at all, but the illegitimate son of a beautiful Spanish woman who had been escorted to the city of Charleston, South Carolina, on October 3, 1803, by a Captain Gorrie, a Spanish Navy or Army Officer, and that his mother had simply adopted the name "Gorrie" for both her and her son. It was reported by some sources that Dr. Gorrie suspected his real father to be of royal heritage. There exists confusion, but October 3, 1803 is the most frequently reported date of his birth. It was known that he was a baby, somewhere between the ages of one and one and one-half when he and his mother moved to Charleston, South Carolina, from Nevis. There has never been any mention of him having a sibling. If Dr. Gorrie's personal, patient, and research records had not been accidentally destroyed, there would probably have been more details about his childhood available. While this may mean that he had been born earlier than October 3, 1803, it is widely accepted that October 3, 1803 was Gorrie's official birthdate.

There are no records indicating that Dr. Gorrie ever had a middle name at all. Interestingly enough, Gorrie Elementary School in Tampa, Florida, is actually named "John B. Gorrie Elementary School." The Hillsborough District School System was questioned regarding the source for the initial "B" in the school's name and school board administrators have no explanation for this. There would have been no concern that Gorrie Elementary School would be confused with John Gorrie Jr. High School, as John Gorrie Jr. High School was built long after Hyde Park Elementary School's name was changed to John Gorrie Elementary School.

Some sources report Gorrie was born in Charleston, South Carolina, but, based upon his physical characteristics (Spanish-looking, with olive complexion, dark hair, and dark eyes) it is more likely that he was born in Charlestown, Nevis. An early biographer wrote a letter to the Crown Official of the British Island of Nevis, an attempt to find out if there were any birth records available on John Gorrie. No records were found. This doesn't mean he wasn't born there, however, as records, in this day and age, were often incomplete or missing entirely.

It doesn't appear that Dr. Gorrie's birthplace was sometimes reported as Charleston, South Carolina, simply in effort to be proclaimed a U.S. citizen, because the 14th Amendment on birthright citizenship (meaning you are a U.S. citizen if born in the United States) was not ratified until 1868—long after Dr. Gorrie passed away in 1855. In March 1790, Congress passed "an act to establish a uniform Rule of Naturalization," which established that children born to American men abroad or at sea were still considered "natural born citizens." Captain Gorrie was, reportedly, at sea when John Gorrie was born.

According to some, it is believed that Gorrie's mother traveled from Spain, during her pregnancy, to the island of Nevis, where she gave birth to her son. At this time, the American Revolutionary War between Great Britain and the 13 American colonies had already taken place. Young Gorrie was a baby when he and his mother moved to Charleston, South Carolina. A naval officer, Captain Gorrie, became a father figure to John. This man was a Scots officer (a captain) serving in the Spanish Navy. Captain Gorrie may have actually been Dr. Gorrie's biological father, as he somewhat supported him, financially and otherwise, until Gorrie reached his last year of college. It is reported that financial support was "cut off" during his final year of college, and this caused great hardship for young Gorrie. Legal records cite a woman named Martha in South Carolina who left a sum of $500 to John Gorrie (later suspected to be her stepson) in her will.

Gorrie's mother had a "Spanish" appearance, and her speech was Creole, indicating that she probably came from the island of Nevis, or was perhaps a slave, brought into South Carolina from the West Indies. If she was single, Gorrie probably lived alone with her in a Charleston, South Carolina household.

It has also been reported that he was the son of William Gorrie, who was living in Richland, County (Columbia) as late as the 1820s. In an 1820 Census, William Gorrie lists a son named John Gorrie, who would have been 16 that year.

It appears Gorrie himself may have been trying to conceal the real story related to who his parents actually were. According to Gorrie's granddaughter, he was of Scotch-Irish descent. To add to this confusion, a Franklin

County (Florida) census shows that Gorrie listed his birth date as 1804 and his birthplace as Charleston, South Carolina.

There is also record of a John Gorrie who lived in Newberry County, South Carolina who listed his heirs as Daniel, Claiborne, Isham, Nathan, Eli, and John. In his will, he left property belonging to his wife, Martha, to his five sons and a sum of $500 to a stepson, John Gorrie. This story may explain the woman named Martha cited in the legal records earlier.

John Gorrie's family, whoever that included, settled in the Dutch Fork area of Charleston, South Carolina. They lived in a log cabin and dealt with the harsh reality that life wasn't always easy or safe. Corn and tobacco were grown and bartered to supply the needs of the family. The South Carolina region endured harsh battles of the American Revolutionary War but victories were few. No doubt Gorrie met many soldiers who would soon have their names on tombstones. Gorrie may have witnessed serious injuries sustained during the war; this may have also been a contributory factor to his interest in medicine, years later.

The fact that John Gorrie was educated in the finest private schools in the Charleston area would mean that the family financial situation was better than most, however. As a young adult, up to about the age of 21, Gorrie worked as an apprentice at an apothecary, something akin to today's pharmacies, for a very well-respected Dr. Green, who also served as the local postmaster. It was during this time that John Gorrie likely became even more interested in the professional practice of medicine.

Dr. Green and Gorrie often referred to *Edinburgh Pharmacopoeia*, a manual similar to today's *Physician's Desk Reference*, which was kept on their countertop. This huge book contained information on every known treatment or cure of the day that could be compounded or made available to a sick person. While working for Dr. Green, Gorrie acquired a broad knowledge of biological products made from plants and animals. He learned of medicinal uses for various metals, as well. The pharmaceuticals of the day were elixirs, pills, and powders. Some of these treatments and cures were effective, some not. While medical knowledge can be shared almost instantly today, communication during this era was very slow in comparison. It could take quite some time for one scientist or physician to learn of the positive research and accomplishments of fellow colleagues.

At the apothecary, Gorrie spent his days doing many chores of an un-skilled nature, like housekeeping, but he also executed duties of a more professional nature with actual patients, even though Dr. Green's schedule left little time to offer pharmacological or medical instruction or to super-vise him. Gorrie's professional duties with patients included "bleeding" (a procedure where blood is allowed to flow from the body from the veins), purging (a treatment for ailments of the gastrointestinal/digestive tract where emetics were administered that caused vomiting), and vermifuging (deworming). Each of these procedures was believed to cleanse the body and restore health and well being. Additionally, Gorrie "kept" the books, collected fees, and assisted Dr. Green with his U.S. Post Office duties. Later in life, Gorrie's experience with postal duties proved valuable in Apalachic-ola, Florida, when he became the postmaster.

It was during these years, working as an apprentice in an apothecary, that John Gorrie witnessed events that would forever change his life; these events would later become his purpose for life. Each warm season, the dreaded fevers of tropical diseases would return, causing many deaths. Some called the fevers "the summer sickness," "the shakes," or "the relapsing kind." In Charleston, South Carolina, alone, yellow fever claimed the lives of 236 citizens in one year. Nearby Columbia, South Carolina, and other south-ern states were in much the same situation. Each day, Gorrie peered out the windows as he worked, witnessing the long procession of horse-drawn wagons hauling the dead to the cemetery for burial.

The signs of death and desperation were everywhere, and fear and panic were a fact of life. Doors, lampposts, carriage houses, and gates were hung with gauze or crape—a sign that patients with yellow fever were on or near the property. Many people burned tar and nitre (the mineral form of potassium nitrate, also known as saltpeter) in the hopes that the fumes would, supposedly, clear the air of the causative agent, although no one actually knew what the actual causative agent was. There was a sickly odor of death all around, and people avoided coming near each other for fear they would be the next fever victim; the mortality rate of both yellow fever and malaria were quite high. Everyone knew of someone who had become sick with the fevers.

Even though Columbia, South Carolina, was the seat of many respected medical professionals, with a thriving Medical Society, there were still outbreaks of tropical diseases in the state—especially yellow fever—year after year. It seemed that very little knowledge was gained with each epidemic. Medical progress was making no inroads on these diseases with relation to preventing the diseases. Most were interested only in curing these diseases, so that is where the efforts were concentrated. There was agreement among medical professionals, however, on several common factors based on when and how the outbreaks seemed to occur: 1) there had been a prevalence of winds over a large area of swamp; 2) outlanders, or those that had recently arrived in the area, were most susceptible to yellow fever; and 3) those of African descent seemed to enjoy a certain level of immunity to yellow fever and became sick less often than Caucasian individuals.

Gorrie himself learned that the standard home treatment for yellow fever—giving the patient a boiled solution of pine top and mullein (a flowering plant)—was often ineffective. Dr. Green's prescription of choice was a substance called "Rush's powder." It consisted of calomel (a compound containing mercury and chloride) and jalop (a compound made of the dried tuberous root of a Mexican plant). This therapy worked in some cases but failed in others and was just as effective in patients as no pharmaceutical treatment. Yellow fever's causes and cures remained a mystery, as medical knowledge was gained very slowly during that time in history.

However, Gorrie observed the fevers became less and less frequent when the weather began to turn cooler each fall. There were no fevers during the winter months. Then, as predicted, the fevers would return at the end of spring, when the temperatures again began to rise. With each new patient, the solution was much the same—treat the symptoms as best you can and hope for a positive outcome. These treatments, of course, didn't increase the survival rates of patients with yellow fever and malaria. Still, physicians of the day tried to learn more as each season of the fevers came and went.

Just as the practice of medicine was different in the 1800s, life itself was also very different, and there were numerous challenges. Water often came into homes by use of a hand pump, outside, or at an inside sink. Sanitation and hygiene were poor; an "outhouse" or a "chamber pot" was used when nature called. Clothes were washed by boiling them over an open fire outside. There were three methods of preserving food: salting, drying, or keeping them in a cool underground cellar. It was not uncommon for people to become ill with food poisoning, especially when food was not plentiful. The choice of available foods varied with the seasons.

There were many popular old wives' tales regarding health and wellness during this time, and some of these tales persist today. For example, people believed that getting "chilled" or sleeping with wet hair caused pneumonia and colds. Many believed handling a toad or touching water that was used to boil eggs would lead to the growth of warts. Raising one's arms overhead during pregnancy was thought to cause a stillbirth or loss of pregnancy. Pregnant women were warned not to consume citrus fruits and juices, as it was believed the acids in these fruits would cause acid "burns" on the baby's face. Additionally, people believed that the fungal infection ringworm was caused by a real worm circling about just under the skin and that head lice infestation was treated by shaving the head. It was also common for parents to believe that "sparing the rod" would indefinitely spoil the child.

Timeline of Inventions in the 1800s

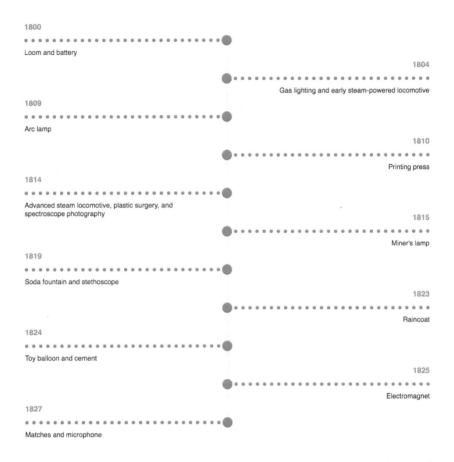

1800

Loom and battery

1804

Gas lighting and early steam-powered locomotive

1809

Arc lamp

1810

Printing press

1814

Advanced steam locomotive, plastic surgery, and
spectroscope photography

1815

Miner's lamp

1819

Soda fountain and stethoscope

1823

Raincoat

1824

Toy balloon and cement

1825

Electromagnet

1827

Matches and microphone

Major Historic Events in the 1800s

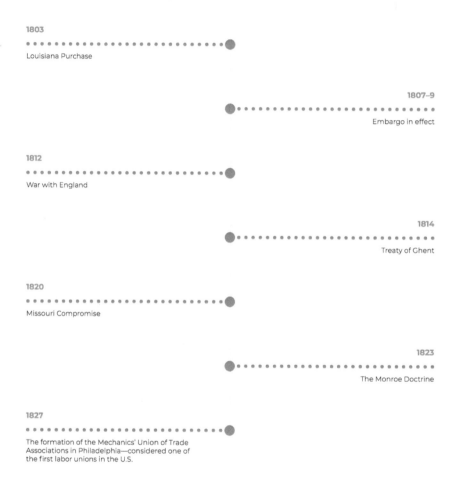

1803

Louisiana Purchase

1807–9

Embargo in effect

1812

War with England

1814

Treaty of Ghent

1820

Missouri Compromise

1823

The Monroe Doctrine

1827

The formation of the Mechanics' Union of Trade Associations in Philadelphia—considered one of the first labor unions in the U.S.

Young John Gorrie was quite intelligent, and he had a thirst for scientific knowledge. Although he respected the knowledge of his colleagues, he was certain that more could be learned if he worked conscientiously. He was quite interested in the recurrent, deadly fevers that came each year as the weather warmed. That, along with other fine qualities, such as empathy, made him an excellent candidate for medical school. The impetus for his pursuit of a career in medicine was very much connected to the suffering he witnessed while working in the apothecary. He knew that there was much to be learned and that something had to be done because it was possible that the entire South would fall victim to these tropical diseases.

Many medical professionals had varied theories about the source and cause of these fevers, and Gorrie wanted to sort all of that out and discover the truth. He wanted to learn all that could be known about treating these diseases effectively and, possibly, curing them, saving millions of lives. Thus, he became determined to enter the world of professional medicine. He endeavored to study under the supervision of the finest medical professionals.

As there were not many medical colleges in the United States, Gorrie's choice of a medical school was not difficult. It is believed that Dr. Green may have persuaded him to choose the College of Physicians and Surgeons of the Western District of New York, also called Fairfield Academy. As time passed, it became quite evident that this institute of higher learning was the very best choice Gorrie could have made. Gorrie was to train under physicians who were among the most respected in the nation. With only a limited knowledge of professional medicine, Gorrie knew of only some of the obstacles he would face. Somehow, he still felt prepared to face whatever would come his way.

—— CHAPTER 3 ——

Becoming Dr. Gorrie

In 1825, at about the age 21, John Gorrie enrolled in Fairfield Academy in Herkimer County, New York. The college had only been open for only a few decades but, having a respected faculty with a challenging course of study, it already had a significant impact on the development of medical science in the United States. By all accounts, this was an excellent medical school for John Gorrie to build upon his interests and earn a medical degree.

Gorrie's name appeared on a list of students attending the school from 1825–1827. Gorrie traveled from his supposed home in South Carolina to Fairfield with great anticipation and, most likely, with a friend, Walker Bean—a student who lived in Columbia. On today's roads, the driving distance totals 931.2 miles! It was, undoubtedly a rough journey, with small trails, many hills, towpaths, and rocky valleys. As his stagecoach, belonging to the Fairfield-Middleville Line, arrived in Fairfield, Gorrie surely felt relief, for this was the longest journey he had ever undertaken and likely the first time he had been away from his mother. Although both Gorrie and Bean were, undoubtedly, quite weary from travel, both knew they would face greater challenges in medical school, where a demanding curriculum would direct their course for the coming years, leaving little time for anything other than learning and studying. This training would require their utmost attention and dedication.

Initially, the curriculum was basic, but, as a result of the Revolutionary War, army surgeons were few and far between. More army surgeons were desperately needed to serve the large and long Canadian frontier. It was for this reason that Fairfield became chartered as a medical school by the New York State Regents. The school added courses in composition, oratory (i.e., public speaking), botany, chemistry, mensuration (i.e., measuring lengths, areas, and volumes using geometry), military art, history, surveying, navigation, astronomy, medical *medica* (a Latin term for the body of collected knowledge about the therapeutic properties of substances used for healing), and more. The college's fine reputation for eminence and popularity was second only to the prestigious Philadelphia Medical School. The scientific and medical history of this learning establishment and its influence on this country are quite impressive, and both endured for some time. Women were not accepted for admission into medical school in this era; medicine was strictly a male profession unless one wanted to be a nurse. Nurses often received their training as they worked on the job, not in a medical training facility.

At this time, individuals would report to Medical School after being granted permission to do so, with a provisional acceptance. The professors would report to the college and begin interviewing prospective students to determine if they were duly qualified (by character, existing knowledge, and interest in the pursuit of professional medicine) to begin medical school. Following these interviews, if successful, a prospective student became an actual student and would begin attending lectures, or classes. John was to interview with the school's vice president, Dr. Westel Willoughby. Medicine, especially long ago, was very reliant upon the Latin language. Gorrie had to impress Dr. Willoughby with his knowledge of Latin and demonstrate a fair moral character. As a Southerner, he was considered to be an outlander, and this, undoubtedly, concerned some. Nevertheless, he must have impressed Dr. Willoughby, as he completed a successful interview for which it is certain he must have practiced beforehand. Very likely, John's ability to think "scientifically" also impressed Dr. Willoughby, for this was considered to be a quality necessary for being a physician.

The college faculty traveled to Fairfield before the beginning of classes, staying for 16 weeks, the duration of the medical lectures. Each member of the faculty would present their curriculum of expertise to the students.

Dr. T. Romeyn Beck pioneered the practice of medical jurisprudence (i.e., branch of science and medicine involving the study and application of scientific and medical knowledge to legal issues). Dr. Westel Willoughby was the professor of obstetrics. Dr. James McNaughton was the professor of human anatomy and physiology.

Gorrie registered for his classes and began his studies under the care of the college treasurer and registrar, Dr. James Hadley, who also served as a professor of chemistry and medical *medica*. Gorrie remembered Dr. Hadley as a real genius; he respected this man of flawless character who combined his knowledge of medicine with botany (i.e., the biology of plants). As Gorrie coursed his way through medical school, he combined his medical knowledge with physics, a subject he was quite fond of.

Gorrie arrived with meager funds, and it took little time for the money-box he had carried from home to be nearly empty. Arriving in October, he quickly paid his tuition, spending $62.50. His lecture tickets would be $54.

Dr. Joseph White, President and Professor of Anatomy and Surgery, introduced the first day of medical lectures. He opened with the statement, "Gentlemen, the profession we have chosen is one of awful responsibility; it gives continued employment to all the processes of understanding and all the kindly affections of the heart … In your studies should be laid a deep and abiding sense of moral obligation." When one looks at Dr. Gorrie's life, it is evident he took these words to heart, adopting a mission to place the common good of the people—his patients and those around him—ahead of his personal desires and worldly gain. The common good of the people, no doubt, entailed health education, and, as his career blossomed, Dr. John Gorrie became one of Florida's first public health educators.

After a long day of orientation, Gorrie retired to his dormitory room, named "Old North." Crude as it was, this room would be his home while he was attending medical school. It was situated on a beautiful tree-lined street. From the window, one could view the foothills of the southern Adirondacks. Nearby would be the home of Dr. William Mather, one of the founders of the school. Chatfield Tavern was not far away, either. South of the campus, one would find the local courting grounds, known as "Cupid's Retreat," where the local village girls enjoyed picnics and dances with the students.

Evident by his accommodations, Gorrie's financial situation was not one to be envied. He brought to medical school only meager funds. In addition to what he had already spent on tuition and lecture tickets, there came further expenses. Dorm room rental would be $14, and, since he needed wood for cooking and heat, he would be required to pay a fee for using the school woodpile. These were not the only costs he would incur, however. He walked down to Kretsinger's general store, down the street from the campus, where he purchased a few dishes, some stationary, and a crock for cooking. While he was provided with a mattress for his cord bedframe, it was empty of the straw needed to make it functional, so he sought out free straw from a local farmer.

Gorrie probably missed the warmer temperatures of the Carolinas when winter came. The climate in New York was quite different. His cold dormitory room was a lonely place. While stimulated by the educational atmosphere of medical school, learning about his things that interested him, he missed the faces of those he cared about; he was homesick, and it was a long way home. It is doubtful that he received any visitors from home. Letters sent from home or to home could take weeks to arrive at their destination.

He missed the friendly faces and familiar life he enjoyed as a youth. He certainly remembered the pungent fogs of his homeland as well. Things were different, now. Published correspondence and diaries of fellow students describe what life was like for Gorrie outside of the classroom. The students went on occasional outings together where they roamed about looking for what they needed to thrive. It's said they stole chickens, foraged milk from cows on nearby farms, and went on maple sugar expeditions, all under the cover of the night sky. These meager findings would be prepared as meals in dormitory rooms, providing a diet of little variety and less than ample nutritional benefit. A visit to the tavern would give the students a place where they could escape the educational atmosphere, if for only a few hours. The next day, however, it was time to be a serious student once again. This was a rigorous course of study, and only the most profound excuses were accepted.

Medical lectures began on the first Tuesday in October and lasted for 16 weeks, with each faculty member traveling to the college from distant homes and other medical schools, settling in for the series of lectures offered that session. Dr. Joseph White was the professor of anatomy and surgery. He was described as "the greatest surgeon in the Western District of New York." Another professor, Dr. T. Romeyn Beck, was regarded as "a star of the first magnitude," having pioneered the science of medical jurisprudence. Yet another professor, Dr. James McNaughton, professor of anatomy and physiology, was known to have a great influence on methods of medical education.

But, it was Gorrie's favorite professor, Dr. James Hadley, whom Gorrie felt was a true genius. He possessed the character and dedication that Gorrie most admired. One of the reasons for Gorrie's great success in medical school was the deep respect he held for his instructors. These individuals were his mentors, and it was his desire to emulate their dedication and professionalism when he became a physician.

Learning about professional medicine meant dissecting human cadavers and observing surgeries whenever the opportunity arose. Gorrie also had his textbooks, which he treasured, referred to, and kept, for years after graduation. Although he didn't know it at the time, one of these textbooks, a physics textbook, would provide vital information for a future endeavor. Gorrie was remembered as one of the most promising graduates of the college. For some unknown reason, however, he lost the financial support of his parents in his final year of medical school. This obstacle proved to be quite difficult, but Gorrie did not let this obstacle deter him from reaching his goal of becoming a physician. He persevered, not only because his professors saw great promise in him but also because he was driven to achieve his goal of becoming a professional physician.

Each student of the College of Physicians and Surgeons was required to write a lengthy thesis as part of the graduation requirements. The thesis was expected to be a detailed and exhaustive report on a challenging aspect of medicine. As graduation approached, Gorrie wrote his thesis on neuralgia, a stabbing, burning, and, often, severe pain due to irritated or damaged nerves. His thesis began with a history of literature on the subject, including its procedure for accurate diagnosis and the probable causes and manifestations of the condition. Gorrie, then, suggested various methods of treatment including the use of cauteries (materials heated or cooled to destroy tissue), and the removal of irritants such as infected teeth or "bad blood." Other remedies included the use of purgatives (medication given to induce vomiting) or emetics (medications given to induce emptying of the bowels), special tonics (nutritional supplements), narcotics (pain medication made from the opium poppy plant, also called opiates), rheumatics (anti-arthritis medications), acupuncture (a type of traditional Chinese medicine that uses tiny, thin needles, inserted through the skin at strategic points on the body), special diets, and certain therapeutic exercises.

Gorrie graduated and earned the title "MD" in 1827, at the tender age of 24. By today's standards, Dr. Gorrie was very young when he graduated from medical school. When you consider how many years medical students attend college in modern times, it is amazing to consider that John Gorrie attended college for only three years! Regardless, the faculty of the College of Physicians and Surgeons greatly admired their graduate, Dr. John Gorrie. Asa Gray was a famed anatomist and an assistant in the chemical department of the college who remembered Dr. Gorrie as a "promising student."

Upon his graduation from medical school, Dr. Gorrie opened his first medical practice in Abbeville, South Carolina in 1828. Just a few years later, in 1831, Gorrie and his mother moved to Sneads, Florida, where he began to practice medicine. His mother became very ill in 1833 and died shortly thereafter. Gorrie, then, made the decision to leave Sneads and move to Apalachicola at the age of 30.

It was springtime when Gorrie arrived in Apalachicola with everything he owned—medical books, some surgical instruments, and clothing. He had learned that Seminole Indians sometimes terrorized the settlers but that Colonel James Gadsden and Governor Duval had persuaded them to move west. As he traveled toward Apalachicola, Gorrie was met with the smell of brackish water along the shores and coastlines. Although Apalachicola was a large port city, there were, in contrast, rows of poorly built storefronts and primitive wooden houses. The location promised a considerable reward to all who made Apalachicola their home. Apalachicola's location, where the river meets the bay, was advantageous for many types of commerce.

The city of Apalachicola was a burgeoning cotton port city on Florida's Gulf Coast, not yet 20 years old. At the time, Apalachicola was the third largest port on the United States Eastern Seaboard. A group of New York merchants, the Apalachicola Land Company, began to purchase large tracts of land adjacent to the river. For nearly 20 years after Dr. Gorrie's arrival in Apalachicola, this same land was unavailable for purchase by others. The Land Company wished to develop the land in and around Apalachicola, so they hired engineers to deepen the harbor. Surveyors were hired to lie out streets, alleys, and parks; carpenters were hired to build wharves so the local merchants could ship goods from their own stores. As the harbor deepened, Apalachicola took her place as one of the great ports of the nation.

At this time, law enforcement was practically nonexistent, so there were accidents, drownings, and brawls in the streets and bars. There were plenty of druggists and empirics who practiced a primitive form of medicine, claiming to be able to cure just about anything that ailed a person. Their treatments were non-medical in nature, for they had no professional medical education. With little knowledge of human anatomy and physiology, their work relied on experience, observation, and experimentation. Although some people trusted them, they were often referred to as "quacks."

Dr. Gorrie hung out his "shingle," meaning he began practicing as a physician, and it wasn't long before he became well respected in the community. It was also in Apalachicola that Dr. Gorrie would later work on his inventions in the fields of air cooling and refrigeration.

There has been almost nothing written about Dr. Gorrie's marriage, other than the fact that she supported his work in refrigeration and ice, but not enthusiastically. I looked and looked and looked. I kept hoping to find out more. While there were times when Dr. Gorrie was very involved in his work, saying very little to others, he attended important functions within the community. Dr. Gorrie was one of the most eligible bachelors in Apalachicola, and he became the first boarder at The Florida Hotel. It was there, in the spring of 1838, that Gorrie became acquainted with his future wife, and he captivated her heart. Her name was Caroline Frances Myrick Beaman.

Caroline was from South Carolina; she had once been married to Henry Douglas Beaman, who was 20 years her senior. She had married him at age 18. On the day that Caroline's son, John Myrick Gorrie, was born, Dr. Gorrie married Ms. Beaman. As there were many questions surrounding his own birth, one can understand Dr. Gorrie's vulnerability at the time, for his mother had faced stigma as a consequence of having born a child out of wedlock. Perhaps he wanted to "make an honest woman" out of Caroline. It is unknown as to whether or not Dr. Gorrie was, in fact, the father of John Myrick. In the meantime, Caroline's family had relocated to Florida in Leon County (Tallahassee). When Henry Beaman passed away, Caroline, at age 32, became a widow, and she made the decision to move to Florida to be closer to her family. Rather than joining her father's household, she decided to live in Apalachicola with her brother and uncle. They had previously entered into business partnerships in Apalachicola. Caroline became proprietress of the Florida Hotel, and a local newspaper, *The Gazette*, recognized her as being an excellent hostess.

The Florida Hotel, managed by the new Mrs. John Gorrie, was very beautiful compared to other such businesses in the area. It was a two-story structure with wide-railed porches and a boardwalk that led to the bay. Spacious rooms with floor-to-ceiling windows kept customers comfortable with breezes that came from the bay. Mrs. Gorrie worked hard to ensure that her patrons had many conveniences not seen in other hotels in the area. Additionally, she was well known for serving the finest foods in the area. Its location allowed patrons easy access to the Post Office, City Market, and the waterfront. Each evening, as his wife concluded her workday, Dr. Gorrie was said to take many late-night walks in the area. It was this time of the day when, uninterrupted, he could think about the things that, to him, were very important in his career and his life.

It is recorded that Dr. Gorrie, then, resigned his various positions in Apalachicola and left the area for a few years. He and his wife returned to the Apalachicola area in 1840, and Gorrie resumed the practice of medicine. Of course, nothing had changed with respect to the yearly fevers. An epidemic of yellow fever in 1841 was so serious that thousands of Floridians died. It was during this epidemic that Dr. Gorrie became even more concerned and more serious about the tropical diseases that came each time the weather became warm. He became more and more determined with each passing day, to end the suffering and death of the fevers. Although there were many different ways to treating these fevers, all of them being medicinal in nature, Dr. Gorrie's strategy would rely on the science of thermodynamics—that of changing the physical properties of the hot and humid environmental air.

In 1845, despite the fact that he was the community physician and that his professional reputation was highly respected, Dr. Gorrie gave up the practice of medicine, permanently, to pursue refrigeration projects. In all likelihood, he probably believed refrigeration projects, and their use in preserving food and curing disease, could save many more lives than he, as an individual physician, ever could.

CHAPTER 4

Florida and the Deep South in the 1800s

A MERICA EXPERIENCED TREMENDOUS growth in the 1800s, and the South was the home of the Confederacy. On October 20, 1803, the United States purchased the Louisiana Territory from France at a price of about 4 cents per acre, a total of $15 million. This doubled the size of the United States and opened up the continent to westward expansion. Seventeen new states were added to the U.S. from 1800 to 1860. For instance, a treaty transferring Florida from Spain went into effect in 1821. Millions of immigrants came from other countries, and they were welcomed. The country had two main parts, each with their different cultures and economies—the North and the South. The Confederate States of America (The Confederacy) was formed in the South with Robert E. Lee becoming the South's military leader. Jefferson Davis was the president of the Confederate States. Africans were taken against their will to America as a commodity to be sold as slaves. Slave ownership was part of life in the South.

Dr. Gorrie wrote, "Devotion to the land has been the Southern man's prevailing habit since the earliest settlement of this country." The South needed slaves to work on the plantations. This was a huge economic issue, because slaves could provide inexpensive labor to farm cotton, tobacco, corn, sugar, and rice. Agriculture was sometimes seen as the only honorable profession. Most slaves lived in the South on vast plantations, although they had no freedom, no formal schools, and no right to vote, as they were not U.S. citizens. The North wanted to free the slaves. The South also wanted strong states' rights, or the right to decide their own government. Wanting to be separate from the United States, the South succeeded from the Union, forming their own new country; the North wanted the country to stay together. The difference in opinions was the cause of the Civil War, which began on April 12, 1861 and ended on April 9, 1865.

The North was industrial, having many factories, railroads, and ports. It was here where much business was conducted and investment capital could be found. This was where the money was—where paper, glass, textiles, household, and metal products for the entire United States were being manufactured. The population of the North was much larger than the population of the South, and the factories employed many immigrants.

Florida became an American Territory in 1821 and a state in 1845. Apalachicola, Florida, is situated in the panhandle of the state, in Franklin County. Apalachicola is an Indian word meaning "the people on the other side." This quaint little town, the county seat, sits near the Gulf of Mexico, where sugar-white beaches greet anyone traveling down the river. The Apalachicola River leads to the Apalachicola Bay, a site of commerce for the city. As one proceeds inland, there is fertile soil, dense woods, and wetlands. Alligators, turtles, snakes, birds, and insects make up the wetland wildlife.

The Apalachicola River's rich floodplains attracted many settlers in the early 1800s, and this played a significant role in the city's development. Apalachicola's location, where the river meets the bay, was advantageous for many types of commerce, promising a considerable reward to all who made Apalachicola their home. As a port city, the opportunities for business activity were many. Apalachicola was a notable cotton distribution center that harbored ships that carried cotton back to Europe and New England. Salt mining was also a prosperous business as salt was necessary for preserving food prior to the invention of refrigeration. Apalachicola was the site of the drafting of Florida's constitution in 1838, although it wasn't until seven years later, in 1845, that Florida became a state. Apalachicola's residents welcomed statehood but knew this designation meant that the country would control the town's commerce and security.

Seminole Indians sometimes terrorized the settlers. Colonel James Gadsden and Governor Duval had persuaded them to move west. This didn't mean that the Seminoles didn't, from time to time, cause difficulties; there were tales of the Indians pillaging, scalping, and kidnapping. Settlers had often moved into Florida under the false assumption that the Indian troubles had been resolved.

Another one of the obstacles for the South was the lack of ice. Without ice to preserve foods, butter, meat, and other foods spoiled within a few days. As a result, it was advantageous when food was in good supply. Ice had to be shipped all the way from Lake Erie or similar sources, and, quite often, it failed to arrive on schedule. The world's first commercial ice plant opened in 1868 in New Orleans, Louisiana. Mississippi followed with the building of an ice plant in Natchez, Mississippi in the late 1870s. A second ice plant, the Morris Ice Company, was opened in Jackson, Mississippi, in 1880.

Most of the shipping business was Northern-owned with all revenue going to Northern pockets. Those working in the shipping industry spent only a few months in Apalachicola each year. This situation disturbed Dr. Gorrie, who wrote the following:

> Under the operation of this system, the city, which in the winter presents the picture of immense business opportunities and vast wealth, becomes in summer, abandoned. All the institutions of civilization are dissolved; the bonds of society are severed, to be revived and repaired in the following winter, but only to be renewed by labor and at the cost of an annually recurring poverty.

Apalachicola, Dr. Gorrie realized, was no different from other seaports in the South, with respect to the economy, that changed with the seasons. The root of this evil, according to Dr. Gorrie, lied in the Southerner's deep attachment to his land, "allowing it to influence all the relations of his life." This leads one to think that Dr. Gorrie's goal of preventing the fevers was related to the economy of the region, not simply the health of the residents.

While Apalachicola was becoming a vital part of the economy in the South, there was a group of citizens frustrated with the Apalachicola Land Company, among other things. Led by Richard Keith Call, they believed they could form a competitive community about 20 miles west of Apalachicola. They called their new town St. Joseph. Gorrie and others thought this effort would be preposterous—way too ambitious for a handful of men, even with the help of a prominent bank. Whatever was to happen, however, St. Joseph was seen as a competitor to Apalachicola. There was also discussion of St. Joseph becoming the new county seat! Apalachicola leaders learned of debate that St. Joseph would become the home of many exceptional businesses that could easily compete with those in Apalachicola, including a hotel comparable to Apalachicola's Mansion House, of which Dr. Gorrie had a financial interest. Fortunately for Apalachicola and its commerce, the impact of St. Joseph was not tremendous, so Apalachicola could continue to progress economically. In 1837, Dr. Gorrie toasted St. Joseph: "to our neighbors, St. Joseph! Competitors in trade, but more successful rivals in courtesy and hospitality. We wish them health and prosperity." This would indicate that any ill feelings regarding St. Joseph were no longer evident. Dr. Gorrie's comments regarding St. Joseph probably eased some of the friction that had existed between the two cities, allowing Apalachicola's city leaders to concentrate on more important issues. The most critical issue for many, especially those that wanted to see the area grow and develop, was the power of the Apalachicola Land Company.

The Apalachicola Land Company was not viewed, by most, as an organization dedicated to economic growth and stability of Apalachicola. In 1838, the company conducted a lot sale, and, at this point, began selling property on credit. This change in the way the company conducted business made it possible for those without cash on hand to purchase property that they could use for business or as a homestead. Dr. Gorrie took advantage of this opportunity and was able to purchase property that he intended to use for his medical practice.

The railroads came to the Apalachicola area in the 1850s, negatively affecting Apalachicola's participation in cotton trade. The state produced much of the beef, pork, salt, and corn for both the civilians and the Confederate forces during the Civil War, but there was a time when a blockage sealed off the harbor. This war strategy stopped the flow of goods to the north, and the result was profound, crippling the local economy.

It was another 10 years until the economy of Apalachicola, and Florida, improved. At this time, the cypress trees in the area became a primary source of income, and the economy prospered. Cypress was harvested for lumber and drilled for "pitch," an oily substance that was used for heating and lamp fuel. Cypress was in great demand as it could be also be used for building many things, including housing and furniture. After 1930, however, because only mature cypress trees were worth harvesting and the species matures very slowly, there was no more cypress available to harvest. Pine and other tree species available in the area did not yield wood products comparable in quality to those made of cypress. The loss of cypress as a resource had an unwelcome consequence for the area. Facing another economic crash, Apalachicola began to use another of its natural resources, the beautiful Apalachicola Bay. Here was a tremendous source of sponges and seafood. Oysters, fish, crabs, and shrimp could be harvested, canned, and preserved. This provided Apalachicola with a new and profitable industry. If ice had been available, as it was in the North, the seafood industry could have provided a much greater source of economic security to the area. Today, Apalachicola leads the state in the sale of oysters and is a chief supplier of shrimp, crabs, and fish, keeping the economy vital.

People will always move toward a location where economic conditions are better and where they can more easily earn a living. When the Apalachicola Land Company refused to sell land, settlers would not come to the area, despite their desire to do so. During Apalachicola's history, there were also other reasons for shifts in population. Native American Indians had resided in Florida for many years before white men arrived, so there were conflicts as settlers moved into the area. Many of these conflicts were a consequence of an inability of these two groups to communicate effectively, and those fearing these conflicts left the area to reside elsewhere. Seasonal changes meant the fevers would come and go, so those that were able to travel to and from the area to avoid infection from the summer sicknesses would do so. Such travel (by river, stagecoach, or otherwise) would be costly. These people who left and returned according to the change in seasons were called "winter robins," but, today, we often refer to them as "snow birds."

For those with nowhere to go—or those whose financial situation did not permit travel to the North to avoid infection—staying in the South was the only option. Each epidemic of yellow fever would result in many deaths. Any city, especially during its youth, would be greatly impacted by the loss of a thousand of more people. The solid citizenry of Apalachicola, those considered to be "real Apalachicolians," stayed in the city year around. These were the citizens who voted in elections and, consequently, had more impact on legislative action.

There was a time when land in the territory was held by the Apalachicola Land Company; settlers coming to the area could not purchase land. This proved frustrating for anyone wanting to relocate to Florida for business or other reasons. It was widely believed that the Apalachicola Land Company had no interest in anything other than earning profits. They had no roots and would simply move on to the next project when they finished with Apalachicola. This all changed when Congress, in 1836, passed a bill that accomplished the following:

> Any man or his legal representative (21 years of age or older) who had inhabited or cultivated any tract of land in the territory, which was not rightly claimed by any other person, would be allowed pre-emptive rights to purchase that land at a price of $1.25 per acre.

When land became available for purchase, people came to the area to plant crops. This was the kind of citizen that Apalachicola needed for growth. When property became available for purchase from the Apalachicola Land Company during the annual land sales, Dr. Gorrie became a property owner.

The "squatters" who didn't actually own land fled the territory, much to the delight of those who actually owned property. The Land Company became quite wealthy, donating $20,000 to deepen the channel (to increase boat travel). This would lead to increased commerce. There was also a donation of money for city improvements, grading the streets and improvements to the Market Square area. The Apalachicola area now had the qualities it needed to attract business and wealth.

In 1841, Apalachicola was at the end of an abysmal cotton season with much cotton remaining unsold. The territory was deep in debt. Prices were high, and money was scarce. Many felt that the secretary of war had not adequately managed the Native American (then referred to as Indians) problem—that being the continued conflict with the white man. The merchants, concerned for their livelihood, were panicked, saying, "There is no solvent or specie paying bank in the territory … this means of effecting internal exchanges at the ruinous losses has paralyzed our industry and rendered it incapable of carrying on business." It was believed that, if the U.S. Senate would confirm the charter for the Marine Insurance Bank of Apalachicola, this would remedy the situation. Gorrie, as one of the charter members of the bank, understood their plea.

Regardless of other challenges, one of the most significant challenges of the South's economy was the fevers. Dr. Gorrie recognized this problem, saying, "Until some cure is found, the poor wretches here and wherever the evil abounds will always be subject to [the fevers'] virulence." In the next few years, Dr. Gorrie's efforts in this area were sometimes welcomed and recognized; other times, his efforts were ridiculed, mocked, and insulted.

CHAPTER 5

Practicing Medicine

THE CHALLENGES of practicing medicine in the 1800s were far different from the challenges seen in modern medicine. Listed below are the notable accomplishments in medicine from 1936 to 1849, when Dr. Gorrie was practicing medicine.

As Apalachicola was a young and growing city, professional law enforcement was practically non-existent. There were accidents, drownings, and brawls; people sometimes required medical attention. Druggists and empirics (individuals who practiced a primitive form of medicine based solely on their observations, not established medical theory) claimed to be able to cure just about anything that ailed a person, from warts to sprained ankles. In many cases, patients simply treated themselves. The local drug store offered good luck "charms," vegetable pills, tonics, and "bitters" all promising to cure a variety of ailments from fevers and ague (malaria symptoms, particularly shaking) to bilousness (indigestion) and dropsy (swelling of the extremities). The Apalachicola Land Company was pleased with

The caduceus is the property of Shannon Martin Sjodin. Picture is also courtesy of Shannon Martin Sjodin.

Notable Accomplishments in Medicine from 1936–1849

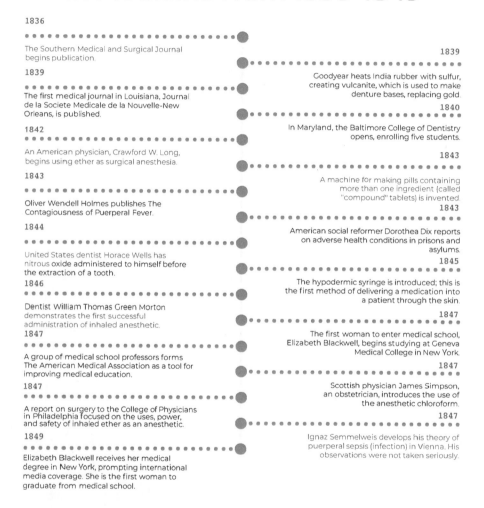

1836

The Southern Medical and Surgical Journal begins publication.

1839

1839

The first medical journal in Louisiana, Journal de la Societe Medicale de la Nouvelle-New Orleans, is published.

Goodyear heats India rubber with sulfur, creating vulcanite, which is used to make denture bases, replacing gold.

1840

1842

An American physician, Crawford W. Long, begins using ether as surgical anesthesia.

In Maryland, the Baltimore College of Dentistry opens, enrolling five students.

1843

1843

Oliver Wendell Holmes publishes The Contagiousness of Puerperal Fever.

A machine for making pills containing more than one ingredient (called "compound" tablets) is invented.

1843

1844

United States dentist Horace Wells has nitrous oxide administered to himself before the extraction of a tooth.

American social reformer Dorothea Dix reports on adverse health conditions in prisons and asylums.

1845

1846

Dentist William Thomas Green Morton demonstrates the first successful administration of inhaled anesthetic.

The hypodermic syringe is introduced; this is the first method of delivering a medication into a patient through the skin.

1847

1847

A group of medical school professors forms The American Medical Association as a tool for improving medical education.

The first woman to enter medical school, Elizabeth Blackwell, begins studying at Geneva Medical College in New York.

1847

1847

A report on surgery at the College of Physicians in Philadelphia focused on the uses, power, and safety of inhaled ether as an anesthetic.

Scottish physician James Simpson, an obstetrician, introduces the use of the anesthetic chloroform.

1847

1849

Elizabeth Blackwell receives her medical degree in New York, prompting international media coverage. She is the first woman to graduate from medical school.

Ignaz Semmelweis develops his theory of puerperal sepsis (infection) in Vienna. His observations were not taken seriously.

Dr. Gorrie's arrival, knowing that a real doctor, a professional man with the skills and training necessary to treat the fevers, would be available to citizens of the area. This was good for their interests. Dr. Gorrie began practicing as a physician and, quickly, he became well respected in the community.

Gorrie settled in, paying $30 a month to rent a long, narrow room in Mr. Darling's Boarding House where it was advertised "no attention shall be in wanting to render the best accommodations for our guests." This boarding house did not, however, provide the comforts found in Charleston hotels, with which he was familiar. The walls were thin, and privacy was uncommon. The boarding house's dining room menu featured bitter coffee, cold biscuits, grits, bacon, and scuppernong (grape) jelly.

Mr. Darling's Boarding House was in the central area of town, and the evenings brought the noise of many rowdy, loud Irish immigrants who were employed by the Land Company. After working long days, the evening was their time to be rowdy; cursing and drinking was their evening enjoyment. Apalachicola's population was transient. Workers would arrive in the winter and depart in the spring. Profits were carried to the North with each departure. Gorrie described it as "the most destructive system of absenteeism that ever impoverished a country." He understood the negative financial impact it had on the community.

The Florida Medical Board had passed a law requiring that any person who practiced medicine in the territory should file, with the Clerk of the Courts in their county, various documents proving competence, including a diploma from a medical college, but these qualifications were not always met. Apprentice physicians sometimes obtained medical licenses as a result of being employed by a practicing physician. Sometimes, "doctors" practiced without a license at all. Regardless of their expertise, however, every medical professional in the area had a very serious and predictable problem—that being the yearly fevers that plagued the residents.

When there were no fevers, Apalachicola was prosperous. The merchants had goods to sell, the staples of life. There was corn, lamp oil, bread, and luxuries such as silk, fine woolens, perfumes, wine, music boxes, and medical supplies such as syringes and lancets. Medications such as aloe, camphor, calomel, ergo, paregoric, and laudanum were also available. "No medicine chest within a hundred miles can match mine for variety and efficacy," boasted Dr. Gorrie. Of course, as the months of the fevers approached, he knew he should stock up on jalop, quinine, and senna root when they were available.

The study and practice of medicine have changed immensely since the 1830s and 1840s, when Dr. Gorrie was practicing medicine. In the 1800s, the leading causes of death were communicable (infectious) diseases, caused by microorganisms such as bacteria, viruses, fungus, and protozoans that, unless present in large numbers, are too small to be seen with the naked eye. Communicable diseases can be transmitted from person to person, and sometimes from animal to human and vice versa. Many died from infection with microorganisms, because medical professionals did not have modern pharmaceuticals such as antibiotics and antiviral agents to fight them. For this reason, the life expectancy of humans living in Dr. Gorrie's time was only about 38.3–48 years. Dr. Gorrie, himself, only lived until age 53, and it is suspected that he died from malaria, a disease that was a primary source of his professional interests.

In modern times, an infected cut or wound can be treated medically, and, often, we become healthy again. Long ago, however, treatments were simple and ineffective. When a person had an infectious disease in the 1800s, the standard treatment procedure was to alleviate the symptoms, pray, or simply "hope for the best." Attempts were made to reduce fever by lowering body temperature using water-soaked cloths. If ice were available, a feverish patient would be placed in a bed filled with ice. It was not uncommon in the early days of medicine for people to be "bled," by a barber or doctor, to get rid of "bad blood."

A vein on the arm would be opened so "bad blood" would drain out, often making the patient sicker. These early medical efforts could not kill pathogenic microorganisms, but, sometimes, the patient's immune system would destroy the disease-causing agent before the patient died. Of course, if infection of a limb would not resolve by using known treatments, the limb would be amputated in effort to save the life of the patient. The first medicine to kill bacterial organisms, penicillin, was not discovered until 1947, and it's a fact that the sore throat or earache you have today could have well caused your death in the 1800s!

In modern times, if there are adequate medical resources to prevent communicable disease, deaths are most often caused by heart attack, stroke, cancer, or injuries due to an accident. These causes of death are non-communicable and are typically linked closely to genetic factors and lifestyle choices. You can't "catch" them from someone else. Medical science continues to advance and, with it, our overall health. Even when a person doesn't make the healthiest of lifestyle choices, we are now able to enjoy much longer lives, because medical professionals have a variety of technologies and pharmaceuticals that can compensate for poor behavioral decisions. For example, the coronary bypass (a surgical procedure designed to improve circulation through the coronary vessels and, therefore, to the heart muscle itself) has saved many lives that would have been lost to heart attacks. Many cancers can be treated successfully by radiation, chemotherapy, surgery, or a combination of these therapies.

The rate at which scientists are gaining knowledge is tremendous. It is a fact that the amount of knowledge gained each year is always greater than the knowledge gained in the previous year. Health educators and medical professionals use this knowledge to teach the public, students, and their patients more effectively. This is another reason why the life expectancy for humans born in and living in developed countries (including the United States) in 2015 was about 78.74 years—much longer than the life expectancy during Dr. Gorrie's day.

Hospitals of the day had no air conditioning or fans to circulate the air. The room temperature in southern hospitals, especially during the warm months, was likely unbearable. Water was brought in by bucket or hand pump, and sanitation practices were unsophisticated. Healthy individuals normally increase their consumption of fluids during warmer weather. Dr. Gorrie's patients would often become dehydrated during the course of the disease, as they were often unable to drink fluids. Adequate hydration is even more important for any person who is sick. Although IV therapy (fluids placed directly into the veins with a hollow needle) was discovered in 1831, it was not widely available until the 1950s. Indeed, Dr. Gorrie's challenge as a physician was huge. Most patients who fell victim to yellow fever or malaria died, despite their physician's valiant efforts. It even seemed likely that a patient could have had yellow fever and malaria at the same time, because mosquitos were (and are) capable of carrying both malaria plasmodium and yellow fever virus at the same time. A person could be bitten by a mosquito that carried both organisms or by more than one mosquito, each carrying different diseases within their bodies. This fact certainly complicated the diagnostic protocol, because physicians of the day had no way to diagnose any diseases through blood testing. Their microscopes could not visualize viral particles. Visualizing virus and plasmodium often required an electron microscope—a type of microscope that has only existed since 1931. Electron microscopes are capable of, at least, 400 times (400X) magnification, and, when they became available, a whole new world of microorganisms came into view.

The quality of microscopes in Dr. Gorrie's day weren't good enough to provide an absolutely accurate diagnosis of any disease that involved microorganisms. As a result, a physician would rely on observations (e.g., a patient's pulse, temperature, respiratory rate, skin color, appearance of the eyes, and response to questions such as when did you start feeling sick, are you able to eat and drink, and do you feel weak?). These observations, questions, and responses were critical, because the human body is subject to many different illnesses. As records were kept, not only to treat the patient in the best way possible but also to learn more, each year (regarding the most effective treatments), this inability to visualize microorganisms "clouded" the data.

Having such a large patient load during the fever seasons made it impossible for Dr. Gorrie to be at every patients' bedside at all times. He cared for patients in his home, at the Marine Hospital, and at the City Hospital. For this reason, it seems likely that Dr. Gorrie's slave, Gus, assisted him by recording important data important to the care of his patients. Dr. Gorrie would have provided specialized training to Gus for this. An important duty of today's medical assistants is keeping patient records, so Gus was probably one of Florida's first medical assistants. Record keeping and data collection are important to any scientific study.

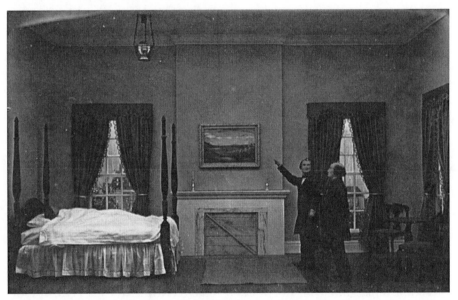

Photo credit: Florida State Archives

Throughout history, it has always been noted that our most outstanding scientists are the ones that are most keenly observant. Some of Dr. Gorrie's patients would first present with symptoms of either yellow fever or malaria, but symptoms of the other disease (if infected with both organisms) would enter "into the picture." Even a scientific thinker like Dr. Gorrie has challenges understanding these epidemics. Fortunately, today, technology enables medical professionals to diagnose more accurately. If someone has a microbial infection, the correct diagnosis may not be immediately known, but it may be known as more tests are completed.

While Dr. Gorrie was most interested in treating those in his own community, it was not uncommon for him to be directed from the site of his medical practice to a health crisis. One March, uncharacteristically early for an outbreak of tropical disease, he received word that a ship, the Magellan, had sickness on board. Although the boat was loaded with goods to be delivered, the crew couldn't bring the ship to port because of the illness. Dr. Gorrie packed a medical bag with the typical medical supplies of the day and traveled, by rowboat, a distance of six miles into the bay. Upon arriving at the Magellan, he found the captain very sick with smallpox. He ordered the ship to hoist a quarantine flag and "let no man go abroad." As he had been exposed to smallpox as well, Dr. Gorrie remained on the ship for 40 days. He wore a mask of gauze when attending to the crew, and, each evening, he would boil it in seawater and hang it out to dry. After the sickness had passed, he insisted the ship be thoroughly scrubbed, with all goods being disinfected before being unloaded on the waterfront. Today, smallpox remains a feared disease with a 33 percent mortality rate, but it has been eradicated, for the most part, worldwide, due to a comprehensive vaccination program.

After Dr. Gorrie and Caroline Beaman were married in 1838, it is recorded that Dr. Gorrie resigned his various public service positions in Apalachicola and left the area for a few years, spending quite a bit of time in New York. It is believed several factors led to this decision. His wife had some business to attend to, and his medical practice wasn't bringing in much money. There was endless haggling over the prices he charged for medical services. Additionally, his income from his work at the Marine Hospital had been cut by 33 percent from the previous year. The City Hospital was overflowing with patients, and the presence of stranded, ill seamen led to pitiful conditions in the streets of the community. It appears that Dr. Gorrie's patience with the situations in Apalachicola was exhausted. Even a professional with Dr. Gorrie's level of dedication found it challenging to carry on.

Dr. Gorrie and his wife returned to the Apalachicola area in early 1840, and Gorrie resumed the practice of medicine. Of course, nothing had changed with respect to the yearly fevers. In fact, an epidemic of yellow fever in 1841 was so severe that thousands of Floridians died. It was during this epidemic that Dr. Gorrie became even more concerned about the tropical diseases that predictably returned each time the weather became warm. With each passing day, he became more and more determined to end the suffering and death from the fevers. Although there were many different ways of treating these fevers, all of them being medicinal in nature, Dr. Gorrie's primary goal was to determine what caused them. Though, most physicians of the day were only interested in learning cures.

Dr. Gorrie became a resident physician at the U.S. Marine Naval Hospital as well as the City Hospital. During one "fevers season," he even devoted two rooms of his own home to treating the sick. It is said that these two rooms comprised the entire second floor of his Apalachicola home; this was quite a sacrifice for any homeowner. All day long, Dr. Gorrie treated those in the hospitals only to come home later to treat the patients in his home.

In 1841, when the season turned to summer, a fever broke out among the workers on the wharf. Soon, others came down with fevers, and a devastating epidemic of yellow fever spread panic through the area. This illness didn't discriminate; anyone was susceptible. Each year, Dr. Gorrie hoped to learn more about the causes for the fevers. Sometimes, scientific knowledge builds slowly. This year, it was thought that the fevers came from three ships that had arrived from Havana, Cuba. Further, it was believed that the previous winter had been too mild, leading to an increased amount of vegetation in the swamps. For Dr. Gorrie, there was ample cause for concern. Dr. Gorrie believed that "man must conquer these morbid woes; he must forge his own weapons as he has in conquering smallpox." It was this epidemic that further strengthened Dr. Gorrrie's resolve to find the cause—not just the cure.

While Dr. Gorrie's primary interest was tropical diseases, he believed man's negative habits also caused disease. Dr. Gorrie encouraged a healthy lifestyle based on healthy decisions. In an early reference to the importance of a healthy lifestyle, Dr. Gorrie said, "Man's very nature condemns him. An attempt to restrain human appetites and passions is as vain and useless as an effort to restrain the tide." This is precisely what healthcare professionals and health educators teach today: that people's lifestyles, in other words, affect the decisions they make day in and day out and determine how long and how well they will live. Almost everyone has the power to make healthy decisions.

Many people believe that heredity is the greatest factor in their wellness, and, because children can't choose their parents, there is nothing they can do but accept the fact that they will probably succumb to the same diseases that affected their ancestors. Today, the world recognizes that a healthy lifestyle, rather than heredity, is a much greater factor in one's health. It is very clear that the factors that dictate quality of life—health, wealth, etc.—are directly related to the decisions people make every day. With age, these decisions become even more significant.

Sadly, because the true causes of yellow fever and malaria were unknown to Dr. Gorrie, the many recommendations (considered to be nonsense today) made to prevent these diseases were not effective in preventing yellow fever or malaria. This was a time when putting garlic in a person's shoes or burning sulfur around their home was thought to prevent illness. The thunderous sound of cannons being shot to "clear the air" of dangerous gasses might not have been the most pleasant way to wake up in the morning.

—— CHAPTER 6 ——

"Tiny Terror"—the Mosquito

WHEN WE THINK of bothersome insects, the mosquito is probably close to the top of the list. Although they are only about 6 mm in length and 2.5 mg in weight, their presence can ruin picnics, camping trips, and other outdoor activities. Humans dislike locusts, gnats, fleas, hornets, spiders, yellow jackets, wasps, and flies, but no other animal on the planet has affected the human race more profoundly than the mosquito.

There are more than 2,500 different species of mosquitoes. These little winged insects have shaped history by spreading/transmitting disease. Thanks to these bugs, countries throughout the world face hemorrhagic dengue fever, filariasis, malaria, yellow fever, Zika, and encephalitis in both humans and animals. Dreaded heartworm infection in dogs, cats, and horses can come from just one mosquito bite, and it can result in the animal's death. Mosquitos have even caused the death of great leaders and entire armies!

Florida, as well as some other southern states, is located in the "subtropics," which means it is close to the equator. In the 1800s and today, much of Florida is below sea level, which is a factor in unique environmental conditions. It is actually believed that Florida was once totally underwater! In the state, one will find many wetlands (swamps) that form the transition zones between upland and deep-water environments. Wetlands are characterized by a seasonal or permanent presence of water. There will also be hydric soils permanently or seasonally saturated with water.

Swamp water is somewhat stagnant; it moves very little, which results in water with low oxygen content (anaerobic conditions). While some organisms, such as certain bacteria, thrive in anaerobic conditions, animal organisms require an environment with oxygen present. The element oxygen (O_2) is part of the molecule carbon dioxide (CO_2), and plants need carbon dioxide to carry out the processes of life. Plants growing in the wetlands (hydrophytic plants) are plants that have adapted to grow in wetland environments. In Florida, hydrophytic plants include tape grass, sago pondweed, Florida bladderwort, coontail, cattails, duck potato, and lemon bacopa.

All living things, including plants, animals, and microorganisms, will grow and reproduce wherever the conditions are the most suitable. Stagnant water is perfect for some plants, and it is also ideal for mosquitos; it makes an excellent breeding ground. Recent evidence suggests that mosquitos can lay their eggs near water quite successfully as well.

As an elected official, Dr. Gorrie educated the public on the dangers of "bad air." Because he believed dangerous gases were formed when swamp vegetation decomposed, he advocated for draining the swamps and removing stagnant water in an effort to decrease the presence of decaying vegetation. This suggestion was not made to reduce the population of mosquitos and, so, was largely ineffective in preventing tropical diseases. This was because scientists and physicians, including Dr. Gorrie, had no knowledge that the mosquito was the vector in the transmission of tropical disease. That fact wasn't proven for 46 years after Dr. Gorrie's death—in 1901. At that time, it was scientifically established that mosquitos carried the plasmodium (protozoan) organism that causes malaria. It was also proven that mosquitos also transmitted the virus that caused yellow fever.

Dr. Gorrie strived to educate the public about food safety as well. Food merchants were often eager to sell their inventory, regardless of quality. In order to earn a profit, perishable foods were sometimes sold after they were no longer suitable for consumption. People would consume food that was spoiled and become ill, particularly during times when food wasn't plentiful. Early microscopes, such as Dr. Gorrie's, were not powerful enough to detect microorganisms present in food products, so food could not be tested for the presence of microorganisms existing in dangerous levels. Only when people could see evidence of contamination with the naked eye would they know it was unsafe to eat. However, millions of microorganisms can be present on a food product before they can be visualized with the naked eye. Dr. Gorrie warned the public about the risk of eating food that had not been properly preserved or stored under optimal conditions.

Dr. Gorrie also educated the public on maintaining a proper lifestyle, encouraging citizens to make healthy behavioral decisions. He warned against heavy alcohol consumption and advised that indiscriminate sexual activity can spread disease. He did not, however, educate the public about the danger of mosquitos, because they were not known to transmit disease. Other medical professionals believed, as Dr. Gorrie did, that tropical diseases were caused by "bad" or "warm" air that originated in the swamps, a consequence of decaying vegetation.

When scientists became aware that the mosquito was capable of spreading tropical diseases, the mosquito became a great cause for concern. The mosquito will always be with us because it reproduces very effectively; they can outnumber people in any given area! Their ability to transmit disease is second to none, especially considering their size and weight, and they do this without becoming ill themselves. Even in these modern times, it is believed that nearly 700 million people, worldwide, become infected with a mosquito-borne illness each year, and more than one million of these victims die.

The mosquito is not an essential food for any other animal, but frogs, birds, lizards, bats, and some fish enjoy them as part of their diet. Other than that, the mosquito does the ecosystem little good. All insects go through similar life cycles in four stages: egg, larva, pupa, and adult. The larva looks much different from the adult insect, and the insect must then go through the pupa stage before it develops into an adult. The adult insect is then capable of reproducing. Consequently, mosquitoes' favorite activities are finding a mate, mating, and reproducing. Mosquitos don't even have a real brain, just a few nerve cells, but those few cells function very well. They have an acute sense of smell, and their compound eyes can sense shadows and light. That's how they find people. In flight, their wings beat 250–500 times per second, but they travel from place to place only at about 3 mph. Only the adult female mosquito can lay eggs and bite. Thankfully, although females need males to reproduce, the males cause no problems. Male mosquitos don't eat blood; instead, they enjoy eating nectar found in flowers.

A female mosquito can bite many people (and animals) as she searches for blood. When a female mosquito bites, she is on a mission. She wants blood, because she needs the nutrients in blood to both make and nourish her eggs. To get blood, she slows her flight and lands on human skin. Then, she seeks out the tiniest blood vessels: the capillaries. She uses tiny, sharp appendages to cut through the skin. This is when humans "feel" the bite.

Next, she injects anti-coagulants and saliva under the skin. The anti-coagulants prevent the blood from clotting. Using her probiscus (mouthparts), she quickly sucks up a "blood meal" (amounting to two to three times her body weight) and then flies away. The victim usually ends up with an itchy, swollen area—all as a result of a small, localized allergic reaction. The itching and swelling will pass within a few days, but, if the bite is subjected to scratching or rubbing, an infection can occur, because many bacterial organisms live under our fingernails and on our skin. Some people are so sensitive to mosquito bites that they develop "skeeter syndrome"—a more-severe reaction that involves blistering and bruising. Mosquitoes bite animals, as well. If a dog, cat, or horse is itching and scratching, their misery may well be caused by mosquito bites, not fleas.

After using the victim as "fast food," the female mosquito is now full. Her next task is to wait for a male mosquito to fertilize her eggs. After a male and female mosquito mate, the female lays 50 to 500 fertilized eggs on the water's surface. The eggs are arranged in a grouping called a "raft" that floats on the surface of the water. A female mosquito can lay eggs up to 10 times during her lifetime; that's somewhere between 500–5,000 eggs, all with the potential to become adult mosquitos. There will be no movement until the eggs mature to the next stage of development.

The fertilized mosquito eggs "incubate" about 24–48 hours, sometimes taking up to 72 hours before hatching, and, when they do, the mosquito larvae "squirming" about in the water is visible to the naked eye. Some people call these squirming larvae "wrigglers." At this point, the larvae spend about 10 days living on algae, protozoans, bacteria, and other organic material, using their mouth "brushes" to take in nourishment. At this point, the mosquito larvae enter the pupal stage, after which it takes about one to three days before the adult mosquito emerges. Mosquitos mature quickly. After another 28 hours or so, this new adult mosquito (if female) can begin biting and breeding. The males start seeking females for breeding.

If the winter isn't too cold, eggs and larvae will not die but become dormant, not progressing to the next stage in the life cycle until environmental conditions improve. Once the weather warms, the reproductive cycle continues. This is just one of the reasons why mosquitos are not likely to become extinct any time soon. It is believed mosquitos have inhabited our planet for 79 million years!

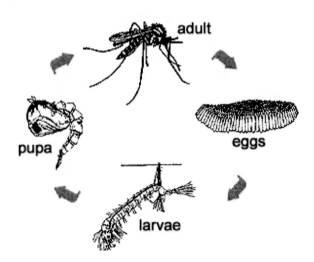

Malaria and yellow fever cannot be spread from human to human by touch or through the air, like colds and influenza. The female mosquito is the vector for, or cause of, infection. Malaria can also infect other primates. The female *Aedes* or *Haemagogus* mosquito transmits the yellow fever virus through bite activity. An uninfected female mosquito becomes infected by biting a person—or another primate—that has the disease. Once infected, the mosquito spreads the infection each time she bites another human or animal.

The more that is understood about mosquitoes, the more the public will be protected from them. Effective mosquito control manages the population of mosquitos, thereby limiting their damage to health. Controlling the mosquito population includes two main areas of responsibility. First, there is individual responsibility. Property owners can maintain their property by keeping a watchful eye on any objects or containers that may collect moisture, such as rainwater. Properties should be cleared of old tires or toys that can hold water. Gutters and drains should be kept clear. Second, governmental agencies have a responsibility to protect residents from mosquitos. These agencies utilize integrated mosquito management (IMM) strategies that include the use of various insecticides/pesticides and proper water drainage. Certain species of frogs, bats, dragonflies, birds, and fish can be integrated into an environment where there is a large population of mosquitos; this can be a positive addition to other methods of control.

Application of chemical insecticides and pesticides, whether by an individual or a governmental agency, involves carefully reading all labels and abiding by the prescribed standards for application. No insecticide or pesticide is 100 percent safe under all conditions; therefore, responsible use is essential, and care must be exercised.

The United States Centers for Disease Control (CDC) and The World Health Organization (WHO) has, as a main interest, controlling the spread of tropical diseases that infect millions around the world. Global health education measures are an important part of their efforts.

CHAPTER 7

Tropical Killers: Malaria and Yellow Fever

THE WORD "EPIDEMIC" strikes fear in the hearts of many. This was especially true in Dr. Gorrie's day when knowledge of microorganisms and effective treatment for illness was in its infancy. The yearly fevers had a high mortality rate, so one can certainly understand the panic and concern. *The St. Joseph Times*, in an attempt to ease public anxiety, reported, "There's been a little sickness here, which almost invariably, has yielded to medical treatment." This was likely reported, because officials in nearby St. Joseph (now called St. Joe) wanted people to believe it was safe to live in the city, because the incidence of fevers was lower. This positive report, however, helped little. Residents in St. Joseph were just as likely as those in Apalachicola were to contract the fevers. As the fevers spread, so did the fear of them. This fear was accompanied by tremendous panic, because these diseases carried with them such a high mortality rate. Since both malaria and yellow fever caused so much suffering and death, one can only imagine the terror that was part of everyday life.

When Dr. Gorrie was practicing medicine, about 50 percent of his patients died. "Until some cure is found," said Dr. Gorrie, "the poor wretches here and wherever the evil abounds will always be subject to its virulence." The summer of 1841 brought a severe epidemic of malaria to the panhandle of Florida, causing the death of 69 percent of the population. Malaria affected, predominantly, the southern states such as Florida and Louisiana, but fewer cases were reported in Texas. Other areas of the country would experience malaria when infected people traveled from place to place. Entire communities would be placed under quarantine, and yellow flags were raised to warn anyone who came near. Those uninfected would try anything they thought would help them to stay well. They would hang gauze over their beds to filter the air and soak handkerchiefs in vinegar and garlic to wear in their shoes. It was believed that soaking bed linens in camphor oil would prevent the fevers as well. Some even advocated shooting a canon or burning gunpowder to clear the air. Gorrie thought these efforts to be trivial and inadequate. Other medical professionals, along with Dr. Gorrie, believed lighting fires were useful in decomposing and dispersing the deadly gasses, or vapors, but it was, at best, a mere substitution of "one impure air for another."

In Dr. Gorrie's day, the world of tiny microorganisms and the role these life forms played in the spread of disease were very mysterious. Scientists believed it was possible that very small living things caused disease, but trying to explain this to others was difficult, as many people did not believe in the presence of any organism they could not visualize with the naked eye. This was truly like fighting an enemy you could not see. Dr. Gorrie had no idea what he was up against. The opinions regarding the cause of these many communicable illnesses and what might possibly cure a person of them were spread far and wide.

As it was not evident how tropical diseases were transmitted from one victim to another, there was no way to stop it. However, there were several theories about the cause(s) of the fevers. Tropical diseases are infectious diseases that occur principally, in the regions of the world closest to the equator. In these regions, summer months feature high temperatures and high levels of humidity. In the wetlands, one can notice a lingering fog that seems to hang over the swamps. The sun steams hotter, and afternoon rain adds more and more humidity, which all contribute to the smell of decomposing vegetation. Gorrie termed these steaming wetlands "morborific" (similar to the term "morbific" today). It was thought by many that these conditions in the swamps were responsible for the transmission of tropical diseases. Though, it was the also the professional opinion of some other medical and scientific professionals that the wetlands had no influence on the incidence of tropical diseases—that they were caused by "badness" (something diseased) within the body. Twenty-five years after Dr. Gorrie died, French surgeon Charles Louis Alphonse Laveran first observed a malaria plasmodium moving within a human red blood cell. For this 1880 discovery, Laveran received the 1907 Nobel Prize in Medicine.

One summer, as an epidemic began to show its ugly head, the *Commercial Advertiser*, a newspaper considered essential to the area, stopped publishing altogether; their printers had left the city. Anyone fearful of the fevers would also disappear, some leaving a note on the door stating, "Gone to Texas." Churches and marketplaces were empty. Little business was conducted—and only by those willing to take the risk of venturing out. Each epidemic caused terror, economic disruption, and thousands of deaths.

In a persistent effort to learn more about tropical diseases, physicians and scientists kept many records (data) to learn more about tropical diseases, but the knowledge was gained very slowly. Additionally, some may have reminded Dr. Gorrie and other researchers that their recorded data might be clouded, unreliable, and of less than optimal value during the next epidemic. Although there has never been any documentation of a patient having both yellow fever and malaria concurrently, this is certainly a possibility, based on what is known about infectious diseases today.

Epidemics often came about when people arrived by ship from the Caribbean, but it was noted that, as long as sailors stayed on their ships, they didn't often become sick with the disease; they somehow had some immunity. It was also noted that heavy drinkers of alcohol, those with liver damage, were more likely to succumb to tropical diseases. Those immigrating recently to southern port cities were the most vulnerable; those that had lived in those same port cities for some time were more resistant to the disease. This was only part of the puzzle that Dr. Gorrie wanted to solve.

Dr. Gorrie grew quite frustrated with his patients' suffering, and, as a humanitarian, he had a great desire to find effective treatments for both malaria and yellow fever. Nevertheless, summer after summer, he would sign a somewhat endless supply of death certificates.

The hospitals of the 1800s were very unlike the hospitals of today. With no air conditioning or fans to circulate the air, the heat was likely unbearable during the warmer months, especially on the upper floors. Patients who already have fevers did not fare well in the warm hospitals. There were no x-ray machines, no laboratories to test medical specimens, no sophisticated pharmaceuticals, and no intravenous fluids. Today, as an infection control measure, nurses, doctors, and laboratory professionals wear masks, gloves, and gowns to prevent the spread of disease. This sort of protection (to patients and to medical professionals) was unheard of as Dr. Gorrie was working to save lives. Modern disinfecting solutions (for floors, instruments, or for the body) were not available. While washing the hands with soap and water is still recognized as an effective infection control measure today, soap was the only product that Dr. Gorrie had available to maintain cleanliness.

The body's normal defense mechanisms (i.e., inducing a fever and increasing white blood cell formation) would begin working when a person became ill with yellow fever or malaria, as the body would sense this microbial invasion. A fever, while uncomfortable, is the body's way to subject microorganisms to high temperatures at which they may not thrive. In some cases, a fever will kill microorganisms that cause disease. White blood cells (leukocytes) are capable of engulfing and destroying many of the microorganisms that can make us ill. Those patients with the strongest immune systems were better able to fight yellow fever and malaria. This may be one reason why some patients recovered while others succumbed to the diseases.

Dr. Gorrie's challenge as a physician was huge! He could often only theorize about ways to help his patients. Many patients who had malaria or yellow fever died, despite any physician's valiant efforts. Some manufactured medicines, whether beneficial or not, were available, but they often ran short in supply when so many patients were in need. When a preferred medication was unavailable, Gorrie relied on native plants, thinking that, "if the forest, swamp, and wood produces the killer, why not the cure?" With experience, Dr. Gorrie observed that a popular remedy for yellow fever, wherein a patient was given a boiled mixture of pine top (a form of turpentine) and mullein (a flowering plant) was ineffective. Yellow fever would also be treated with conventional methods such as purging (administering medications to induce vomiting/diarrhea), and bloodletting.

Another standard treatment prescribed for yellow fever involved boiling a mixture of crushed cayenne and chili peppers and using the water to wash the rash/sores that appeared on the patient.

Indeed, Dr. Gorrie tried everything he could think of to comfort and, perhaps, cure his patients, but about half of them died, anyway. There were no fever-reducing medications such as aspirin, acetaminophen, or ibuprofen to lower body temperature and make a patient more comfortable. The primary treatment for malaria was the administration of quinine, a type of salt. Adding salt (sodium) may have helped the patient maintain a normal blood pressure and blood volume, but, because the destruction of red blood cells kills the patient, it was not a cure for malaria.

Whenever someone would recover from these illnesses, it was often thought "nature had worked the cure" and the treatments were not the primary reason why the patient survived. Today, though, scientists understand that mosquitos, as seen in the chart below, transmit both malaria and yellow fever. If Dr. Gorrie had understood this, his strategies for preventing infection would have been quite different.

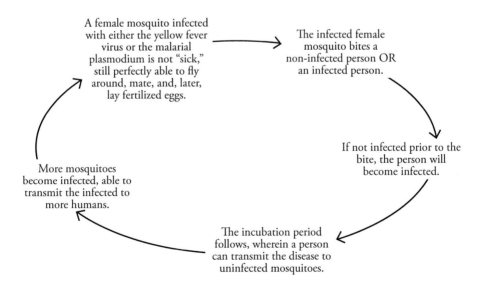

Yellow Fever

Yellow fever is believed to have originated in the jungles of South America as a virus that affected only primates (man, monkey, baboon, chimpanzee, etc.). Before 1822, yellow fever attacked cities as far north as Boston, but, after 1822, it became common only in the South. Port cities such as Apalachicola, Florida, were primary targets, but the disease occasionally spread up the Mississippi River in the 1800s to citizens in New Orleans, Mobile, Savannah, and Charleston.

Once a person is infected with the yellow fever virus, there is a three-to-six day incubation period in which the patient feels well and experiences no symptoms. After the incubation period has passed, however, the disease enters stage one, the acute phase. During this phase, a patient will experience high fever, severe headache, muscle aches (particularly in the back and knees), sensitivity to light, nausea and vomiting, loss of appetite, dizziness, and red eyes, face, and tongue.

After stage one, one of two things happen:

1) A patient's symptoms resolve, and the patient survives.

2) The patient's symptoms worsen, and the patient enters stage two—the toxic stage.

In the second stage, the acute signs and symptoms from the first stage return. More severe and life-threatening symptoms also appear, such as yellowing of the skin and eyes (jaundice), abdominal pain, vomiting with or without blood, reduced urination, bleeding from nose, mouth, and eyes, decreased heart rate, liver and kidney failure, delirium, seizures, and coma, which is indicative of brain malfunction. It is during this stage that the patient dies.

Viruses are not capable of reproducing on their own. They cannot divide through cell division (mitosis) as many other cells can. To reproduce and spread infection within the body, the yellow fever virus, like all viruses, seeks out a host cell once it enters the body. Then, the virus attaches itself to the host cell and injects its genetic material into the cell. After that, the cell is no longer what it used to be—becoming, instead, a vehicle for the manufacture of new viruses. As the number of viruses in the body increases, the patient becomes sicker. This parasitic relationship is similar to one of a candy bar company breaking into another candy bar company's factory, and then using the machinery to make their candy bars.

Eventually, a cell becomes so full of new viruses that the cell's plasma membrane breaks open—through a process called lysis—and the newly made viruses are released into the body, where they, in turn, seek out their own host cell. Their sheer number can overwhelm a patient's immune system, causing death.

Yellow fever only kills 10 percent of its victims today; it was much more deadly in the 1800s. Because it is a viral illness, the only thing that can be done is to alleviate the symptoms and comfort the patient; there are no specific treatments for the disease. In the United States, humans are the only known primates to become infected with the yellow fever virus. The disease is most common in areas of Africa and South America, so it is wise to consult your doctor if you are traveling to those areas; you may be advised to get a yellow fever vaccine to prevent infection. The vaccine has a high rate of effectiveness.

Malaria

In Dr. Gorrie's day, malaria was recognized as a disease that brought great misery and death. Those infected with malaria usually developed symptoms within 10 to 15 days of being bitten by a mosquito that carries the parasite. It is caused by a microorganism called *Plasmodium*, a type of parasitic protozoa. Once in the body, *Plasmodium* uses the victim's liver cells as hosts for maturation, where it will continue to divide and make more of itself (mitosis) and grow, moving into other areas of the body as the blood moves through the body.

The first symptoms of malaria (i.e., nausea, fever, headache, and chills) may be mild and difficult to recognize as malaria. Then, 24 hours later, as the parasite destructs red blood cells, severe anemia (a lack of red blood cells) occurs. Red blood cells (erythrocytes) contain the hemoglobin molecule (containing proteins and iron) that enables them to "carry" carbon dioxide and oxygen. Without enough red blood cells, the blood cannot carry oxygen and carbon dioxide adequately, so the body's cells are starved of oxygen. Further, carbon dioxide (a waste product) is not removed from the cells as it should be, and carbon dioxide builds up in the body. This causes respiratory distress, and the patient's respiratory rate increases dramatically. There is a change in the pH of body fluids as acid wastes build up in the body (this is called acidosis). Without rapid medical treatment, acidosis results in multiple organ failure. Death soon follows.

Malaria is thought to be responsible for approximately one to three million deaths per year, with 80 to 90 percent of the deaths being in rural sub-Saharan Africa. The World Health Organization cites malaria as the world's fourth leading cause of death in children younger than 5 years old.

Today

While antibiotics can be useful in treating many bacterial infections in modern times, diseases caused by viral and parasitic organisms must be treated with specialized pharmaceuticals that may be unavailable in many areas of the world. One of the greatest achievements in medicine, intravenous (IV) therapy, was not discovered until 1831. IV therapy has advanced and is now a standard of care for many hospital patients, particularly those that cannot inject fluids or food. Such therapy would have, undoubtedly, saved the lives of many of Dr. Gorrie's patients. Of course, poverty, war, and other economic and social instabilities in endemic regions are still obstacles to preventing and treating tropical diseases.

Another remarkable achievement in medicine, which saves many millions of lives today, is vaccines. During Dr. Gorrie's day, vaccine use was in its infancy; there were few vaccines, and their use was not widespread. There was no vaccine available for either yellow fever or malaria. In the case of many diseases, such as smallpox and polio, a vaccine provides immunity for life. French physician and scientist Louis Pasteur (1822–1895) invented the chicken cholera vaccine, the anthrax vaccine, and the rabies vaccine. English physician Edward Jenner (1749–1823) discovered a process of vaccination using the cowpox virus to provide cross-immunity to prevent smallpox.

Vaccines are a way to use weakened or dead pathogens (germs) in a liquid serum, to provide immunity to disease. The patient receives the serum, usually, by injection. Immunity to a disease is achieved when the body's immune system is tricked into believing it has been exposed to the live pathogen. The immune system responds by producing specific antibodies (protein molecules) that fight the particular pathogen contained within the serum, but the immunity produced protects against the real pathogen as well as the weakened version of it.

Today, yellow fever and malaria can be prevented by vaccine, although the malaria vaccine has a low rate of effectiveness. It is wise to consult your physician before traveling to affected areas to determine if you should be vaccinated before beginning your journey.

Physicians of today have almost unlimited access to research completed by other physicians and scientists. Professional medical organizations in each branch of medicine meet on a regular basis to share research and ideas. Professional publications such as medical journals and medical research studies are shared among members. The United States' Centers for Disease Control (CDC) and the World Health Organization (WHO) are always available to share the latest achievements in medicine. Further, the CDC's website enables the public to access health advice regarding a wide variety of illnesses.

CHAPTER 8

John Gorrie, the Public Servant

FEW CAN SAY they contributed as much to their local community as Dr. Gorrie did. His tireless efforts brought about many positive changes for the Apalachicola community. Of course, a physician who arrives in a location where he is sorely needed quickly makes a positive impact on his community, but a great deal of what Dr. Gorrie did was directly related to positions he held that were not medical in nature. Dr. Gorrie had a real sense of public servitude, and he was a true humanitarian. These values may have been learned as a result of rigorous upbringing in private schools or from his mother, but, most definitely, the medical professors he trained under impacted his character. They were highly respected, and they certainly imparted the value of public service upon Gorrie.

By the time the John Gorrie arrived in Apalachicola, in 1833, the town was already flourishing as the third largest port on the Gulf (following New Orleans, Louisiana, and Mobile, Alabama). Apalachicola harbored ships carrying cotton to Europe and New England. Many probably stayed away from the area due to the fevers that came during the summers, but tropical diseases were of great interest to Dr. Gorrie. He knew he could be of service to the public if living in the Apalachicola area. It wasn't long before he became active in the community.

Not long after Dr. Gorrie arrived in Apalachicola, a local newspaper learned of his concern for public health, especially concerning sanitation practices. The editor of the local newspaper, *The Gazette*, asked Dr. Gorrie for a statement addressing his concerns. Gorrie agreed to provide such a statement:

I consider it of first importance, he advised, that the present wharves be removed … and a solid line built from the highest to the lowest point required by the commerce of the place. The new wharves (piers) would not be filled with wood or mud but with stone ballast.

He also suggested the dry culture of the low grounds surrounding the margin of the bay, "not by rooting up all vegetation in sight, for growing plants that are the means by which nature purifies the air." Lastly, he warned the following:

The proprietors may drain and fill up every wet place within miles of the city; the city may advise and enforce a rigid medical police, but, unless every citizen lends a hearty concurrence and assistance, malarial complaints will prevail. Local causes, always adequate to the production of endemic fever, are, to the great majority, the sole cause.

Although the mosquito was not known, at the time, to be the vector for these tropical diseases, Dr. Gorrie also recommended mosquito netting (gauze) be hung over sleeping areas as a way to prevent these diseases.

Dr. Gorrie was, first and foremost, a physician. As a physician, he had an obligation to respect the rules of this honorable profession. The rules encompass the Hippocratic Oath. All physicians take this Oath when they graduate from medical school and are expected to abide by it. The administration of the Hippocratic Oath remains an important part of the all medical school commencement ceremonies today.

Although there have been various versions of The Hippocratic Oath over the years, it always goes something like this:

I swear to fulfill, to the best of my ability and judgment, this covenant:

"To hold him who taught me this art equally dear to me as my parents, to be a partner in life with him, and to fulfill his needs when required; to look upon his offspring as equals to my own siblings, and to teach them this art, if they shall wish to learn it, without fee or contract; and that by the set rules, lectures, and every other mode of instruction, I will impart a knowledge of the art to my own sons, and those of my teachers, and to students bound by this contract and having sworn this Oath to the law of medicine, but to no others.

I will use those dietary regimens which will benefit my patients according to my greatest ability and judgment, and I will do no harm or injustice to them.

I will not give a lethal drug to anyone if I am asked, nor will I advise such a plan; and similarly I will not give a woman a pessary to cause an abortion.

In purity and according to divine law will I carry out my life and my art.

I will not use the knife, even upon those suffering from stones, but I will leave this to those who are trained in this craft.

Into whatever homes I go, I will enter them for the benefit of the sick, avoiding any voluntary act of impropriety or corruption, including the seduction of women or men, whether they are free men or slaves.

Whatever I see or hear in the lives of my patients, whether in connection with my professional practice or not, which ought not to be spoken of outside, I will keep secret, as considering all such things to be private.

So long as I maintain this Oath faithfully and without corruption, may it be granted to me to partake of life fully and the practice of my art, gaining the respect of all men for all time. However, should I transgress this Oath and violate it, may the opposite be my fate"

(Translated by Michael North, National Library of Medicine, 2002).

Dr. Gorrie was obligated to abide by this Hippocratic Oath and, by all appearances, he did, even as he assumed public duties. Of great significance to Dr. Gorrie's story is his assertion that he "will prevent disease whenever [he] can, for prevention is preferable to cure."

In the early 1800s, physicians had difficulty earning a living, because there were no health insurance companies to guarantee payment when a patient received medical services. Gorrie's patients, unless at a government healthcare facility, were self-pay; in other words, the patient had to pay for each service as it was rendered. However, not everyone could pay, and, sometimes, rather than paying for medical services with money, patients paid their doctor with a chicken, jar of jam, some bacon, or a bottle of lamp oil. Of course, no one can meet their financial obligations with these items, so Dr. Gorrie had to find additional employment in Apalachicola to earn a sustainable living. Many such professionals often supplemented their income with positions of public service.

Shortly after Dr. Gorrie arrived in Apalachicola, he met Dr. William D. Price, an established physician and member of the Territorial Medical Examining Board—now called the Florida Medical Board. Price was also Apalachicola's postmaster, an appraiser for the Union Bank, and a customs inspector. The salary he earned as postmaster was $200 per year. Dr. Price wrote a letter to the U.S. postmaster general saying he was inclined to surrender (resign from) the postmaster's position "because of the malignant fever that prevailed five months of each year; all [residents] who are able abandon the area during the sickly season." He added that, "having known this, [he] would never have been induced … to continue at all seasons at the peril of [his] own life."

Gorrie's appointment to the position of postmaster in November 1834 was as an assistant to Dr. Price. During the summer months, Dr. Price would leave the area, leaving Dr. Gorrie in charge. Dr. Gorrie earned $131.20 per year as assistant postmaster. One of the most essential duties of this position was to publish *The Advertiser*, a publication listing the names of those who had letters waiting at the local post office. Gorrie later replaced Price as postmaster, remaining in that position until 1838.

The job of postmaster had one great advantage, however. The small mail-room offered privacy when he needed it. Further, this room became a place where he could meet influential members of the community. Conversations with other professionals—including lawyers, judges, preachers, and agents of all kinds—provided an opportunity for him to learn what was going on in the local areas that Gorrie chose to avoid and miles around where he didn't travel at all. On some days, captains of ships would bring notices from plantation owners in Georgia, offering rewards for the return of runaway slaves. There was frequent mention of Indian depredations. Most of the discussions, however, concerned the Apalachicola Land Company, often referred to as "money-grubbing opportunists." Gorrie, like many, had hopes that President Jackson would do something about the Land Company; his appointments of citizens to public office, however, left a lot to be desired.

Each day, Dr. Gorrie took a leisurely stroll on the outskirts of town. The townspeople took notice of this soft-spoken man—a man of quiet habits. Gorrie sometimes paused to look out over the bay, and people wondered if he was simply inclined to daydreaming or if he had he experienced a deep sorrow or some other unfortunate event. In truth, Dr. Gorrie was dreaming about mankind and the world he lived in. For, each May, it seemed as if the entire city packed its bags and boarded the steamers heading north. Most everyone agreed that the dangers of the fevers, the summer sicknesses, were too great. Left behind were only the "unfortunates," residents who were forced to stay behind by necessity. No one could blame those that wanted to escape the expected epidemics.

In 1835, Dr. Gorrie was appointed as a Florida Notary Public. He ran for a position in, and was elected to, the Apalachicola City Council. The City Council certainly had great respect for him, because they later appointed him as council chairperson and city treasurer. Then, he served as vice inten-dant (vice mayor) in 1836 and became intendant (mayor) on January 22, 1837. Many would not have been interested in the mayoral position, as the city had little resources for paying public officials. In only two short years, Dr. Gorrie's public responsibilities changed quite a bit. The first thing Dr. Gorrie did as mayor was sit at his desk and pen a letter to Apalachicola's

City Council. He was filled with purpose, calling attention to his qualifications for serving as mayor, but, most importantly, he wanted to make clear his aims for the upcoming year: "I am willing to serve, provided I be endowed with the necessary powers and means for maintaining the peace, for increasing the public health, and for advancing the internal improvement for the city." He made it clear that he expected to have the resources to do his job well.

As mayor, Dr. Gorrie found himself in a position to begin his lifelong advocacy of public health. As a physician, he had no real platform with which to influence the public. As mayor, he hoped to maintain an effective platform. As a first priority, Gorrie hoped to persuade those able to provide money to build a public hospital that would serve indigent citizens, perhaps through a poor tax. There were other changes he wished to make as well. For years, he had been disgusted at the sight of meats and fish rotting in the markets. Fruits, surrounded by flies, way past ripeness were equally upsetting. Dr. Gorrie felt that, unless all-around conditions improved, there was no real reason for him to serve as mayor. In the position of mayor, he became a public health educator, not with that title, per se, but knowing it as part of his duty. He was one of Florida's first public health educators. Although the city hospital was not completed and open for business until Dr. Gorrie's time as mayor ended, it was through his efforts that the hospital came into existence.

Sanitation (including food safety, sewage systems, and infection control) was rarely a part of life in the South, and illness related to this situation was far too frequent. In addition to the fevers, summer brought standing pools of water and raw sewage in the streets. Some jobs were left undone. There was the unwelcome smell of discarded oyster shells in the marketplace. Debris and trash sent down the river for disposal were stuck in the natural vegetation where they decomposed. Dr. Gorrie's annual plea was to clean up the streets, drain the swamps, clear the weeds, and maintain clean food markets in an effort to improve the health of local citizens. He offered advice to anyone who would listen, but, mostly, he wanted to impress upon the influential that public health could be improved by a collaborative effort. There was one bold push to clean up Apalachicola, as Dr. Gorrie recommended, but, as time passed, the efforts waned.

There were some successes in response to Dr. Gorrie's public health concerns and the public health education he afforded the community. The city council passed an ordinance requiring regular inspection by the city marshal. The markets would be open only from daybreak until 10 a.m. with no meat being allowed to remain in the market after closing hours. A second ordinance provided that all cotton on the wharves must be taken off within two days of its arrival. This ordinance was not favored by those who were negatively impacted by the strict schedules. The expense of hiring additional workers to meet the requirements of the ordinance was unwelcome.

As mayor, Gorrie was frequently called upon to attend meetings, funerals, appraise estates, and serve as a Master of Ceremonies for social functions. In addition to his responsibilities as mayor, Dr. Gorrie's had his private medical practice and postmaster duties. A dinner to celebrate the incorporation of the Marine Insurance Bank of Apalachicola was held, and Gorrie was one of the bank's directors. In 1837, Dr. Gorrie was asked, and agreed, to preside over the inaugural ball for newly elected President Van Buren, which was quite an honor. Later that year, Dr. Gorrie's attendance was requested at a dinner to honor the homecoming of the Franklin Guards following their encounter with the Seminole Indians. With no consideration, it seems, to the limits of Dr. Gorrie's schedule, Gorrie took on more commitments when the city council appointed him the attending physician at the city hospital.

Dr. Gorrie was also on the founding committee of the local Masonic lodge. The primary purpose of the Masonic organization was to make "better men out of good men." There was, and is, an emphasis placed on the individual man by strengthening his character, improving his moral and spiritual outlook on life, and broadening his mind. Gorrie's fellow lodge members selected him to be secretary of the lodge in 1835.

Serving as president of the Apalachicola Branch Bank of Pensacola in 1836 was another milestone in Gorrie's service history. In 1837, he also became a charter member of the Marine Insurance Bank of Apalachicola. In 1841, he was named as Franklin County's justice of the peace. Although Dr. Gorrie was not a profoundly religious man, he did take part in the founding of Apalachicola's Trinity Episcopal Church in 1837. Dr. Gorrie's name is listed in church records as a charter, or original, member of the congregation and founding vestryman (church officer).

Once the returning Franklin guards informed the group that the war was no longer merely close to Apalachicola—it had arrived—he became a resident physician of the Marine Hospital Service of the U.S. Treasury Department, working from 1837–1844. His patient load was quite large. It was at the Marine Hospital that Dr. Gorrie set up his first air-cooling systems. Cooling a patient's room involved positioning ice above patients' beds, near the foot of the bed. As air flowed over the ice, the temperature of the air surrounding the patient dropped. A hole in the floor allowed the air to exit the room.

His interest in the commerce of Apalachicola led him to the presidency of the Apalachicola Branch of the Bank of Pensacola, and he was a charter member of the Marine Insurance Bank of Apalachicola. Dr. Gorrie was also a managing and financial partner in the Mansion House Motel, a site of important meetings and social events in the city.

In 1838, Dr. Gorrie resigned the office of mayor. It is thought there were several reasons for this decision. Firstly, an anonymous letter, written by a 33-year-old citizen, was published in the *Courier*. The letter made allegations that there were serious issues surrounding a loan that had been secured by the city. Some even speculated that Dr. Gorrie himself may have written the letter. Secondly, Gorrie's granddaughter, Sarah Robinson, once stated that he resigned to devote more time to his professional duties as a physician. Lastly, his resignation could have very well been related to the fact that he was in a relationship with Caroline Beaman. She hadn't been a widow very long when she and Dr. Gorrie became much more than friends.

Dr. Gorrie's tireless efforts brought about many positive changes in Apalachicola. He believed diligent scientific work, including medical research, would benefit mankind, possibly saving millions of lives, and he wanted to be a part of that. He believed, also, that public health education was of utmost importance to the health of a community. This may be what fueled his motivation. In many ways, this research consumed him. However, when alone, not working with the public, he was a quiet man of very few words.

CHAPTER 9

Using the Scientific Method to Find an Answer

D R. GORRIE NOTED, "Nature would terminate the fevers by the changing of the seasons," and, when the weather cooled in fall, winter, and spring, the incidences of malaria and yellow fever dropped to virtually zero. Therefore, he theorized it was "bad air," very warm air, from the wetland areas, that caused the illnesses associated with the fevers, and many others agreed with him. Dr. Gorrie didn't really know why this "bad air" caused disease, although he utilized logical reasoning and the scientific method to come to what he thought was the answer. Dr. Gorrie was able to rely on his microscope for some observations, but early microscopes were not capable of magnifying the smallest of microorganisms; he was not able to visualize the organisms that caused these tropical diseases. We now know that the air, the wetlands, and the mosquito are all intertwined in the story.

Even though several historians/authors have not recognized Dr. Gorrie's efforts in health education, it is clear that he was quite interested in public health education and believed he could make a difference. Dr. Gorrie believed that a person's lifestyle (the decisions a person makes as they go through each day) plays a significant in their health. It made sense to Dr. Gorrie—if people practiced a healthier lifestyle, they would be less likely to become sick. He would often remind others that overeating, and over-drinking lessened resistance to disease. "All diseases," he claimed, "stem from three principle causes—atmospheric impurity, contagion, and debauchery." The word *debauchery,* meaning excessive indulgence in sensual pleasures, was likely used in reference to the sexually transmitted disease known as syphilis. Syphilis has plagued mankind throughout history, and it is transmitted through sexual activity. In Gorrie's day, there were no antibiotics to treat a patient infected with the bacteria that caused syphilis.

To further educate the public about the dangers of the fevers that were sure to come each year, Gorrie assumed the pen name "Jenner" and published a series of 11 articles under the title *On the Prevention of Malarial Diseases* that appeared in the *Commercial Advertiser*.

As a resident at the U.S. Marine Hospital in Apalachicola, where yellow fever and malaria were prevalent during the warmer months, Dr. Gorrie noticed that his patients seem to suffer more during the warm nights, as fevers are often higher during the evening hours. He felt that the ravages of these fevers could be controlled and relieved by cooling the air, so he turned his attention to the development of a method of ventilating a sick room with cool air, as a method for the prevention and treatment of fevers. Dr. Gorrie viewed this mission as a matter of medical necessity—an urgent need to cure his patients of a disease he thought was caused by the extreme heat and humidity. While he was working on the issues surrounding tropical diseases, other inventors were working on the blueprint, the stapler, the grain elevator, mercerized cotton, the sewing machine, the pneumatic tire, and anesthesia of various types. Each of these inventors was rewarded, financially, for their work.

"A questioning mind, seeking out the secrets of medicine and science, would be given the answer to the riddle of the fevers," said Dr. Gorrie. And, deep in his consciousness lay a deep conviction for finding that answer and, given the time and means for the search, he would find it.

While conducting research on the causative agents of tropical diseases was his primary focus, Dr. Gorrie had many patients to take care of during the fever seasons. Trial and error, along with careful record keeping, were of benefit. He worked diligently to find effective treatments and cures for the fevers, relying, somewhat, on his mentors—fellow physicians he met while in medical school and elsewhere—whom he'd admired and respected. He also paid attention to the various observations and suggestions found in professional medical journals. Dr. Gorrie felt, very strongly, that cooling the air would not only comfort his patients and ease their symptoms, but it may possibly kill any suspected disease-causing organisms carried in "bad air," so he theorized that cooling the air might be a way to rid the air of the agents causing the fevers.

In addition to being a physician and public health educator, Gorrie was also an inventor and a scientist. Therefore, he often employed the scientific method when working to solve a problem. The scientific method is an organized procedure wherein a hypothesis is either proved or disproved. The steps of the method are as follows, but there are many variations in the verbiage:

1. State the problem in the form of a question.

2. Research the problem.

3. Develop a hypothesis (i.e., a preliminary answer based upon research and observation).

4. Develop an experiment to test the hypothesis.

5. Conduct the experiment.

6. Record data from the experiment.

7. Develop a conclusion.

8. Share your results with others.

Dr. Gorrie's method, when executed, probably resembled the eight steps listed above. First, he recognized and identified the main problem he faced: why did people in the tropical and subtropical areas of the world experience fevers each year as the weather warms? Next, Dr. Gorrie began researching the problem by communicating with other industry professionals. He studied any published material regarding the diseases and kept records each time he treated a patient, noting whether the patient succumbed to or survived the disease. Although not reported, he also likely kept records of weather conditions, including temperature, that might be related to the occurrence of disease.

Then, Dr. Gorrie, as well as other scientific professionals, developed the hypothesis that very warm air (and decomposition of the vegetation in the local swamps) caused the fevers and that cooler air would both comfort his patients and lead to a higher rate of survival. It was felt the "causative agent" formed when decomposing vegetation released "bad air." To test his hypothesis, Dr. Gorrie developed an experiment that cooled the air in rooms with sick patients. He suspended ice above patients' beds, waiting for it to cool the air.

While his experiment progressed, Dr. Gorrie would observe his patients, as per usual, recording data on each patient who was cared for in the cooled rooms which likely consisted of adults and children alike. That data included his sensory observations and the patients' temperature. Dr. Gorrie probably had a fairly accurate method of measuring patients' temperatures, since he has access to thermometers similar to those we use today. Inventor Gabriel Fahrenheit was inspired by thermometers of the 1600s that used alcohol to measure temperature, and, in 1714, Fahrenheit invented a more practical thermometer that used mercury, rather than alcohol. Fahrenheit's thermometer could measure body temperature within a reasonable amount of time. Soon after, medical student Anton de Haen developed a more practical thermometer that became popular among medical professionals. It was capable of measuring body temperature, either orally or rectally. Haen's thermometers were likely the ones used by Gorrie.

Although all of Dr. Gorrie's records, including research data, were accidentally destroyed during the Civil War, it is assumed that he observed the typical survival rates, regardless of the air temperature, because warm air did not actually *cause* malaria and yellow fever. However, there may have been a higher (or lower) rate of survival merely as a coincidence. If there had been no indication that air cooling would increase patient comfort and rates of survival, Dr. Gorrie would have probably not have made the decision to move forward in inventing a machine that made artificial ice.

Consequently, the world benefitted from his findings, despite their inaccuracies. Coincidence or not, Dr. Gorrie developed the conclusion that cooling the air could lead to increased patient comfort and an increased rate of survival in those afflicted with yellow fever and malaria. Although scientists are encouraged to share their data and conclusions with others, Gorrie likely shared this information with only a few individuals, because many felt his ideas were outlandish; he didn't want to subject himself to humiliation from those that didn't understand his interest in cooling the air.

Dr. Gorrie believed that, if he tried hard enough, he could build some sort of machine that could make artificial ice, and, if he succeeded, he could save millions of lives throughout the world, as many areas were known to have epidemics of yellow fever and malaria. Further, cool air (what we call refrigeration) would prevent or delay spoiling of perishable foods. This was important because, without refrigeration, food spoiled very quickly. Food poisoning was not uncommon in the 1800s.

Although Dr. Gorrie, and many other scientists and physicians, hypothesized that wetlands, decaying vegetation, and warm air were the reasons for the yearly fevers, the mosquito was not actually proven to be a vector (the organism responsible for the transmission) for both yellow fever and malaria until decades after Dr. Gorrie's death.

Many would say he was consumed with learning how to cool the air in patient rooms. He also understood that reducing the humidity was necessary as well. He found the answer to this issue in Neil Arnott's *Elements of Physics*. Condensing four cubic yards of air into the space of one cubic yard would reduce the ability of that air to hold moisture by 75 percent.

It was in the sick wards of the U.S. Marine Hospital, and in the sick room behind his home office (called the "Fever Room") that the very first process of air conditioning, or cooling air, was invented. Gorrie's first room-cooling system, wherein ice was suspended from the ceiling, was a passive process rather than a mechanical process; it relied on the casual movement of air over a container of ice, not an air compressor. Because it was not mechanical in nature, it couldn't be counted upon to work at any given moment.

For this first cooling system (ice suspended above beds), Dr. Gorrie knew he needed large quantities of ice to cool the air with some degree of efficiency. The fevers came about during the warmest months of the year, and ice would melt quite quickly in increased temperatures. This was only part of the problem, however, because, in the South, ice was extremely difficult to come by. Ice shipments would come down the Mississippi River on steamboats, or across the Atlantic Ocean, on ships. Even when it could be purchased, in the coldest months of the year, it was quite expensive, costing as much as $5 a pound (about $29.55 a pound today). Even if it had been affordable, ice was not available during the hot summer months. If ice were delivered during the warm months, it wouldn't have lasted very long in the heat. Gorrie foresaw it would be possible for the ice companies in the North to trade ice for cotton, rice, tobacco, and sugar. After all, the South had plenty of these commodities to spare, and the North had plenty of ice.

After much thought about how to secure an unending supply of ice, Dr. Gorrie decided he needed to find a way to make ice artificially. He believed, "through hard work and dedication," it would be possible to *make* ice. No other physician, inventor, or scientist that he knew of was interested in this mission. Physicians studied many branches of science in medical school, and Dr. Gorrie recalled a branch of physics called thermodynamics, which involved the temperature of matter and how it can produce energy. He reviewed the concepts of thermodynamics that he had learned in medical school. According to thermodynamics, the air in our atmosphere can exist in several densities, and, when air expands, it becomes cooler, like one encounters when climbing high mountains. In high altitudes, the air is less dense (lower air pressure), so it is cooler. Conversely, when air is compressed, as when a heated cooking pot is closed, the air becomes warmer. Using this knowledge, Dr. Gorrie began his new mission—to make artificial ice.

Some would say that he worked too hard on this new project. He was very driven, keeping to himself for long periods of time, not speaking to anyone else. He would often take long walks to think, relax, and relieve stress. Dr. Gorrie's research, however, was limited by the era. It is believed that he owned a vast library of books from his youth and from medical school. Surely, these books were often the only resource available to him as he worked in his laboratory. His laboratory was crude by today's standards. He concentrated on the concepts of thermodynamics for days on end without breaks, but it seemed to be impossible for a person to expand air. *What would he have to do to expand that cubic foot of air?*

Just as he was going to give up hope, it occurred to him that, maybe, the way to expand air was to first compress it. He knew that compressing air (decreasing its volume) would warm it. If that same air is released under pressure, through a small opening, it would then expand, and, according to the principles of thermodynamics, its temperature would drop. This is precisely what happens when you push the button on the top of an aerosol can; the compressed air in the can is released through the tiny opening, and what comes out—whether only air or a solution containing air—is always a lower temperature than the contents of the can. Water freezes more quickly in high mountain elevations, so he believed it was possible to expand air enough to make ice. *Could Gorrie develop such a system that would expand air enough to freeze water into ice?* The only way to learn the answer to that question was to build such a system, a machine that could compress and release air. Certainly, his motivation increased tremendously, because he'd had an idea that he believed would work.

Dr. Gorrie was the first to utilize the air compression process as a method of cooling air. Though, in 1799, long before Dr. Gorrie even thought about compressing air, England's George Medhurst invented an air compressor for mining. Soon, the world would realize the full potential of air compression.

CHAPTER 10

Dr. Gorrie's Cool Solution

I N ORDER TO pursue his interest in artificial ice, Dr. Gorrie made the decision to leave the practice of medicine in 1845. As one of Apalachicola's most respected physicians, and as a steadfast humanitarian, this departure from medicine must have been difficult for him. He remained on call, however, and was rarely paid for professional services. This was a man with great conscience and tremendous compassion; he was known to put others before himself. He obviously felt that air-cooling would do more for mankind than he could do as an individual.

Dr. Gorrie was determined to invent a machine that could make artificial ice, and his departure from the practice of medicine provided him with the extra time he needed to work on his goal, however outlandish it was considered to be. Hecklers in the Apalachicola area and elsewhere mocked his aspirations. If that wasn't bad enough, one New Yorker wrote, "There is a crank down in Apalachicola, Florida, a Dr. John Gorrie, who claims he can make ice as good as God Almighty." This negative attention did not deter Dr. Gorrie, although it must have embarrassed him when others did not believe his goal was attainable. There are always those who will discredit others and those that will discourage the aspirations of others. Many millions of people have benefitted from his inventions, though, because Dr. Gorrie's ambitions were much stronger than the negativity that seemed to surround him.

Dr. Gorrie felt it was possible, through scientific effort, to remedy the evils of humidity and high temperatures. He thought if houses in the North were built to keep out cold, why couldn't houses in the South be built to keep out heat? Why couldn't some mechanical means be developed for lowering temperature and extracting moisture from the air?

He knew that, when a liquid evaporates into a gas, it does so at a specific temperature, which varies depending on the type of gas and the amount of pressure it is under. As that same liquid evaporates, the liquid extracts heat from the surroundings. Likewise, when a gas is compressed, it is heated; when the pressure is removed, the gas expands because it absorbs heat. Gorrie thought, if the air were highly compressed, it would heat up by the energy of compression. If this compressed air were run through metal pipes cooled with water, and, if this air was cooled to the water temperature and expanded down to atmospheric pressure again, quite low temperatures could be obtained, possibly low enough to freeze nearby water in pans.

He wrote down his ideas for the project and then began making preliminary drawings of what would become his ice machine. Soon, Gorrie's preliminary drawings led to more complex designs. Eventually, he produced a final drawing that he would use as a model to build his multi-chambered ice machine.

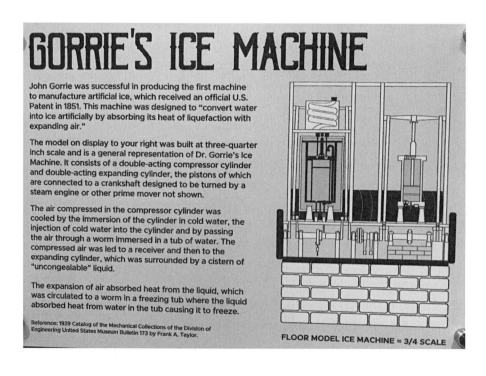

GORRIE'S ICE MACHINE

John Gorrie was successful in producing the first machine to manufacture artificial ice, which received an official U.S. Patent in 1851. This machine was designed to "convert water into ice artificially by absorbing its heat of liquefaction with expanding air."

The model on display to your right was built at three-quarter inch scale and is a general representation of Dr. Gorrie's Ice Machine. It consists of a double-acting compressor cylinder and double-acting expanding cylinder, the pistons of which are connected to a crankshaft designed to be turned by a steam engine or other prime mover not shown.

The air compressed in the compressor cylinder was cooled by the immersion of the cylinder in cold water, the injection of cold water into the cylinder and by passing the air through a worm immersed in a tub of water. The compressed air was led to a receiver and then to the expanding cylinder, which was surrounded by a cistern of "uncongealable" liquid.

The expansion of air absorbed heat from the liquid, which was circulated to a worm in a freezing tub where the liquid absorbed heat from water in the tub causing it to freeze.

Reference: 1939 Catalog of the Mechanical Collections of the Division of Engineering United States Museum Bulletin 173 by Frank A. Taylor.

FLOOR MODEL ICE MACHINE = 3/4 SCALE

This was remarkable, as paper only provides two-dimensional images. His machine was a three-dimensional machine made of wood and metal, and he was a physician, not a carpenter. He would need to secure the tools and materials from various sources. Wooden boards, screws, nails, metals, a saw, a hand drill, a hammer, and more were needed. Gorrie built his ice machine over several months. Finally, the construction was complete. While not a wealthy individual, Dr. Gorrie began spending nearly all of his time and money in the hopes that his machine would work.

Gorrie's ice machine consisted of a pump that compressed air into a small spiral pipe. That compressed air was forced through a small opening, which, in turn, expanded it. Dr. Gorrie hoped that this expansion of air, increasing the volume of the air, would cool the air enough to turn the water stored in partially filled metal barrels into ice. When the machine was set into motion, Gorrie discovered his hypothesis was correct. His machine worked! The cold air cooled the water in the metal barrel to a temperature of 32°F, which changed the water's state from a liquid to a solid. He had made artificial ice!

This first ice machine and the manner in which it functioned laid the groundwork for all modern refrigeration and air-conditioning. This is why Dr. Gorrie is considered a pioneer, and it's also why Dr. Gorrie is recognized as the father of refrigeration and air conditioning. The ice machine in home freezers, supermarkets, restaurants, and convenience stores are all modeled after Dr. Gorrie's original ice machine. Although Dr. Gorrie didn't invent modern air conditioning, he did invent the central functioning component of all modern machines that cool air! In the 1840s, however, it was not possible to connect Gorrie's ice machine to an electrical outlet as a source of power. Therefore, it was necessary to find a source of power (energy) for his air compressor (pump) to work. In his patents, Gorrie suggested that this pump could be powered by horse, water, wind-driven sails, or steam power. Though electricity and gasoline power modern machines, it is impossible to ignore Gorrie's contribution to science. Additionally, machines are relying more heavily on wind and thermal energy—greener sources of power similar to the ones Gorrie suggests using in his patents. Today, the original model of Dr. Gorrie's ice machine and the scientific articles he wrote in support of his invention are housed in the Smithsonian Institution in Washington, DC.

Dr. Gorrie submitted a patent application for his ice machine to the U.S. Patent Office on February 27, 1848, three years after Florida became a state. He was granted the first U.S. patent (number 8080) for mechanical refrigeration on May 6, 1851. Once patented, the ice machine could be mass-produced without any concern that someone could copy the machine's design and receive a financial reward from Gorrie's invention.

Before the issuance of the patent, Dr. Gorrie likely shared information about his invention with only a few trusted individuals. Quite naturally, he feared that, if someone else learned of his work, they might be able to capitalize on it. He did confide in his friend and colleague, Dr. Chapman, who then asked him, "Have you managed to freeze your patients?" Dr. Gorrie replied, "No, but I have made ice!"

Dr. Gorrie's ice machine was first publicly demonstrated in June 1850. Apalachicola's beautiful Mansion House, which he co-founded, was holding a banquet to celebrate Bastille Day and required Gorrie's new device. The anniversary of the storming of the Bastille fortress in 1789 was a turning point of the French Revolution. July 14, 1790, is also the date of the Fête de la Fédération, which celebrates the unity of the French people. The Mansion House Hotel, being the second largest hotel in Florida, was widely respected as the site of the most prestigious events in the area. The French Consul, Monsieur Rousard was in attendance. Champagne was to be served, and the Consul expected the champagne to be chilled. He also knew, however, that it was the month of June and ice was very difficult to come by, if one could find it at all. At that moment, there was no ice available in Apalachicola, and there wouldn't be any for quite some time. Monsier Rousard mentioned this issue to Dr. Chapman, who was in on the secret demonstration. Dr. Chapman told Monsier Rousard that, "as a surprise to the guests, the wine would be chilled."

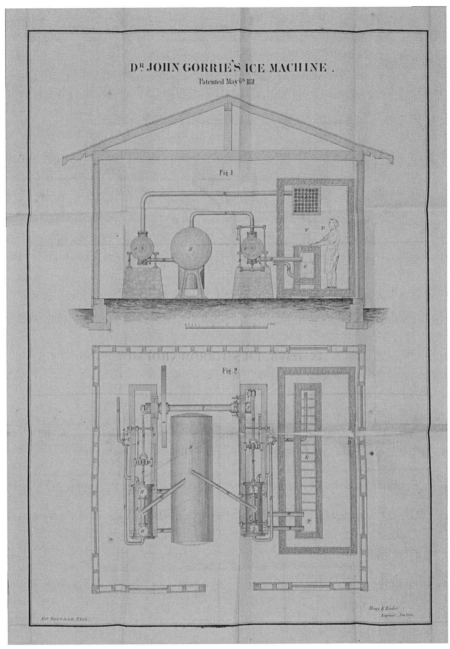

Photo credit: U.S. Patent and Trademark Office

And so, Monsieur Rousard was able to say to his guests, "For my dinner, I will have *ze* ice." When the time came, waiters entered the banquet room carrying baskets of champagne covered with ice as well as silver platters loaded down with ice cubes. The guests were amazed. They applauded vigorously! Many congratulations were extended to Dr. Gorrie for his pioneering work on a machine that could manufacture artificial ice.

Gorrie had used air as the working gas in his machine. He took his idea to a northern company, Cincinnati Iron Works, which created a model for public demonstration. The company built one of the first ice machines for Dr. Gorrie in 1848, after which Dr. Gorrie, in October of 1848, demonstrated its operation. This event was described in *Scientific American* in September of 1849. Although the process of making artificial ice with Dr. Gorrie's machine was slow (taking up to eight hours to produce a barrel of ice), leaked water, and was inconsistent, the machine was capable of producing ice in large quantities. In 1868, the first commercial ice factory in the world was built in New Orleans, Louisiana, utilizing Gorrie's invention.

Dr. Gorrie's Scientific Method:

1. State the problem: how can I make ice artificially?

2. Research the problem: Dr. Gorrie reviewed the principles of thermodynamics and rediscovered a key concept—when air is expanded, the temperature drops.

3. Develop a hypothesis: Dr. Gorrie supposes that, if he can expand air enough to drop the temperature, he can freeze water.

4. Develop an experiment: he eventually determines that compressing air and releasing it into a larger area—in small increments—will expand air.

5. Conduct the experiment: Dr. Gorrie invents and builds a machine that first compresses air and then expands it. After many weeks spent building the machine, Dr. Gorrie tests the machine.

6. Record data: Dr. Gorrie observes that his machine works. He writes down the data.

7. Develop a conclusion: Dr. Gorrie concludes that it is possible to make ice artificially.

8. Share results: Dr. Gorrie submits paperwork/application to patent his machine.

---- CHAPTER 11 ----

Dr. Gorrie's Dreams Die with Him

I N HIS FINAL months of life, It became very important to Dr. Gorrie that the new patent he had applied for, the patent for a mechanical air conditioning process, a "cooling and disinfecting ventilation," unlike the ice machine, would be solely *his own*. He hoped this new invention would reestablish his credibility in the world of scientific medicine when the commercialization of his ice machine had miserably failed. In the winter of 1855, he visited the local post office almost daily, eagerly looking for any correspondence from the U.S. Patent Office. News regarding this latest patent for air conditioning was months overdue, and Dr. Gorrie was concerned that another inventor, without his knowledge, had already patented a similar process.

Dr. Gorrie was a brilliant scientist and inventor—the first to utilize an air compressor to cool air. All previous cooling systems relied on more primitive methods. It was his ingenious use of an air compressor that made his ice machine work.

An air compressor is a mechanical device that uses a motor to convert power into compressed air, as a form of potential energy. The air compressor forces air into a chamber able to endure the pressure of the compressed air, and, later, that air is forced out as a form of kinetic energy (energy from motion). The use of an air compressor was critical then, and it continues to be critical today; air compressors are the primary functional component of all modern machines that cool air.

Air compressors can supply kinetic energy that helps with many everyday tasks. They are used to fill propane cylinders, air mattresses, and tires. Even manual bicycle pumps use a small air compressor operated by a handle. An air compressor is what powers pressure washers, nail guns, and jackhammers. They are also used to supply an undersea diver with a consistent supply of air. One would be accurate when they say that Dr. Gorrie was the "father" to many other inventions besides refrigeration and air conditioning.

After securing his patent for the ice machine, Dr. Gorrie went to New Orleans to visit prominent individuals who might be interested in his ice machine. He also met with similar executives in the investment capitals in the North. He needed capital (money) for commercial production, but, like anyone attempting to market a device, he needed to lay a foundation for product demand. In the North, ice was abundant, and its presence was taken for granted. In the South, ice wasn't viewed as an actual necessity; it was considered to be a luxury.

Dr. Gorrie was not an impractical dreamer; he simply did not possess the ability to help others see what he could see. He was not a businessman, and he was not a salesman. After spending nearly all of his money to make the ice machine, as well as traveling extensively in search of investors, Gorrie was left penniless. In response to the low consumer demand, Dr. Gorrie wrote the following:

> I propose simply to place it in the power of every man to lower the temperature below the hydrometric moisture and [cleansed of the miasma,] that portion of atmosphere actually used by him in respiration, during the period of danger from malaria by the refrigerative, condensing, and disinfecting agency of ice.

When some people heard the news about a machine that made artificial ice, they were astonished, and some simply could not believe it was true.

Although his chief aim was to improve conditions for the sick, he envisioned commercial use for his product. Those very close to him understood and appreciated his work, but, whenever Dr. Gorrie mentioned his ice machine to most, it was easy to see that they were disinterested. Dr. Gorrie was unable to help potential investors visualize the vast possibilities and importance of his work. Try as he might, Dr. Gorrie did not always appear credible to others—possibly because the issues he recognized did not affect others to the magnitude that they affected the South. Further, those not educated in the field of medicine would not understand the possible implications his research posed for human health.

Sadly, there are always those who will resent the aspirations and successes of others, sometimes aggressively, sometimes passively. These people probably shed "a bad light" on Dr. Gorrie. Dr. Gorrie was disrespectfully ridiculed and heckled for his work by those that simply knew no better. With his invention being ridiculed regularly in the press, any potential investors became disinterested. Dr. Gorrie cited this as a moral obstacle to his success. It is not hard to imagine how this type of ridicule could make one feel isolated and depressed.

Perhaps the greatest obstacle to Dr. Gorrie's success in marketing the ice machine came from the ice lobby. A close eye was being kept on Dr. Gorrie's work, as it was considered to be a substantial threat to the livelihood of those in the ice industry. In 1805, Bostonian Frederic Tudor (1783–1864) began harvesting ice in the winter from frozen rivers, ponds, and lakes in the North. This became the North American natural ice trade. As a result of his success, Tudor was quite powerful and compelling as the man behind a "smear" campaign against Dr. Gorrie and his invention. Tudor's equipment, as well as the process of distributing ice to all who needed it, were very costly. Tudor had a tremendous amount of money invested in the industry. The less-expensive source of ice produced by Dr. Gorrie's machine was a threat to Tudor's empire, for he had had a monopoly on the ice trade since 1827. The ice industry was an enormous industry. By the year 1847, nearly 52,000 tons of natural ice traveled by ship or train to 28 U.S. cities. It was about 1900 before ice harvesting ended and ice machines were counted upon to make ice. By this time, Dr. Gorrie would have been 45 years old.

It was in 1868, 13 years after Dr. Gorrie's death, that the world's first commercial ice plant opened in New Orleans, Louisiana. Mississippi followed with an ice house being built in Natchez in the late 1870s. Shortly after that, a second ice plant was opened in Jackson, Mississippi, owned by the Morris Ice Company.

Unfortunately, because John Gorrie was not a businessman, he was forced to sell half to three-quarters of his interest in the ice machine to a business-man from New Orleans. This potential investor died unexpectedly, prior to providing any funds to Gorrie. Gorrie's financial situation worsened when he was sued by a London debt collector for unpaid interest in the amount of $6,500, a considerable sum of money for the time. With his invention being ridiculed regularly in the press, other potential investors became dis-interested. It seemed that, if it weren't for *bad* luck, Dr. Gorrie wouldn't have had any luck at all.

In his eyes, and in the eyes of others, Dr. Gorrie suffered such tremen-dous failure that it is not surprising that his health was negatively affected. Having always been very goal-driven, he was devastated when no further avenues were available for his inventions. Many say he suffered a nervous collapse (mental breakdown). Undoubtedly, Gorrie must have been de-pressed, embarrassed, and extremely disappointed. It is easy to imagine how humiliated and hopeless he must have felt.

When last seen, Dr. Gorrie was sitting on his upstairs front porch, wrapped in a blanket in June of 1855. It is said that he died from malaria—a disease he hoped to find a way to prevent, and to cure, during his lifetime. It is believed that Gorrie knew his death was impending; he had asked his wife to bring paper and pen so he could write out his last will and testament. He wrote out a crude will a few days before his death. This will, as well as a few private records, can be found in Franklin County Official Records. His very thoughtful will, especially considering his failing health, contained several requests. However, his fourth request had the biggest impact on his legacy. He died on June 29, 1855, and the request was explained as follows:

> I give, devise, and bequeath unto my said wife all my interest in and to certain patents granted to or to be granted to me by the United States Patent Office or other patent offices throughout the

world, the one for an artificial process for manufacturing ice of which I have an interest of one-fourth extending all over the earth, the other for cooling and disinfecting ventilation, the interest of which (when granted) will be solely and exclusively my own.

Dr. Gorrie also asked to "rest near the sea" in his adoptive Apalachicola, a gesture of his love for the area. The application of his discoveries to refrigeration and, eventually, air conditioning, lay in the years far beyond Dr. Gorrie's lifetime. He was later reburied in Gorrie Square, the site of the John Gorrie State Park Museum and the monument that was placed, in his honor, by the Southern Ice Commission.

Caroline lived for 11 years after Dr. Gorrie's death but never received any financial reward from her husband's inventions or patents. Caroline wrote a last will and testament with the same request (concerning Dr. Gorrie's patents and financial interests), leaving these interests to her children, and they to theirs. Willis Carrier's inventive efforts began many decades after Dr. Gorrie's death. It is unclear why Gorrie's few descendants were never afforded any financial reward from his patents. Perhaps these descendants were not aware of their rights where this was concerned.

Dr. Gorrie was survived by his wife, Caroline (1805–1864), his stepson, John Myrick (1838–1866), and his daughter, Sarah (1844–1908), who later became Sarah Gorrie Floyd. Captain Gabriel Floyd was killed in battle, but they had a daughter, Carrie Floyd Stewart. Later, Sarah married W. L. Robinson, and they had two children—a son, O. L. Johnson, and a daughter, Mary L. Johnson.

Dr. Gorrie, his wife, and his stepson were buried in St. Luke's Episcopal Cemetery in Apalachicola, but, in 1899, Dr. Gorrie's body was moved a short distance to Gorrie Square in Apalachicola when the Southern Ice Commission donated a beautiful monument/memorial to rest in his honor. Sarah Gorrie Robinson is buried in Milton, Florida. This magnificent monument is a tremendous source of pride for the citizens of Apalachicola and Franklin County.

Dr. Gorrie's funeral featured his bier being carried by Apalachicola's leading citizens. Behind them walked his stepson. Then followed the town population, with many bearing flowers, all interested in a farewell tribute to Dr. Gorrie. His mentor, Dr. Chapman, noted, "There is the grave of the man whom we recognize as superior to us all." Edward W. Bock, another Floridian, expressed this sentiment:

> It isn't love. It isn't brotherhood. It isn't friendship. It is a word that embodies the spirit and the meaning of all three of these words. The word is service. Not the service that serves self … but service in the true and intended meaning of the word—the service that labors for the interest of others.

It is known that Sarah Gorrie once said, "It is with great gratification to me to know my father was the original inventor of the ice machine that has certainly proved of untold benefit to humanity living in hot climates."

Dr. Gorrie concluded that that mechanical refrigeration "had been found in advance of the wants of the country." Decades after Dr. Gorrie died, inventor and American engineer Willis Haviland Carrier (1876–950) somehow secured—or, rather, "seized," according to a 2018 video from the Travel Channel—the information in Dr. Gorrie's patents. Carrier graduated from Cornell University in 1901 with a BS degree in engineering. Carrier's educational credentials were of more benefit (than that of an MD) when it came to the further development of the science of air cooling. Carrier has become recognized for the invention of modern air conditioning, inventing the first electrical air conditioning unit in 1902. Carrier was admirably cited for his invention that would "control temperature, control humidity, control air circulation, and ventilation, and cleanse the air." On January 2, 1906, Carrier was granted U.S. Patent 808,897 for an Apparatus for Treating Air, the world's first spray-type air conditioning equipment. It was designed to humidify or dehumidify air. Heating water was its first function, and cooling it was its second. This design was unlike any air-cooling apparatus developed by Dr. Gorrie.

Photo credit: Florida State Archives

Photo credit: Florida State Archives

On December 3, 1911, Carrier presented a scientifically significant document on air conditioning, "Rational Psychrometric Formulae," at an annual meeting of the American Society of Mechanical Engineers. This document would relate the concepts of relative humidity, absolute humidity, and dew-point temperature, thus, making it possible to design air-conditioning systems. The terms "relative humidity," "absolute humidity," and "dew-point temperature" are frequently utilized in weather broadcasting today.

Carrier had been employed with the Buffalo Forge Company for about 12 years when, around 1914, the company made the decision to prioritize manufacturing. Seven New York engineers joined Carrier (J. Irvine Lyle, Edward T. Murphy, L. Logan Lewis, Ernest T. Lyle, Frank Sanna, Alfred E. Stacey Jr., and Edmund P. Heckel) and pooled their savings together to form the Carrier Engineering Corporation on June 26, 1915.

Surely, Carrier and the other six engineers weren't thinking only of themselves during this enterprise, but these individuals were not the humanitarians that Dr. Gorrie was, as humanitarianism produces little potential for revenue. Carrier, like Gorrie, has also been recognized as an individual who has provided substantial benefit to others. A brilliant individual, Carrier had the opportunity to utilize prior knowledge that was secured by a respected scientist. Carrier initially produced air conditioners for the Westinghouse Company and, later, in 1915, founded the Carrier Air Conditioning Company. However, Dr. Gorrie's legacy endures because, most certainly, Dr. Gorrie completed much of the scientific experimentation that led to Willis Carrier's success.

During the 1939 New York World's Fair, Carrier displayed a structure he termed an "igloo." This provided the public an image of the future as it related to modern air conditioning. After World War II, which ended on September 2, 1945, there ensued an economic resurgence. Modern air conditioning became much more popular and accessible, and, over the coming years, air conditioning became a necessity for modern homes and businesses. Few wished to live or work without the comfort it provided.

The HVAC (heating, ventilation, and air conditioning) industry today, is recognized as a vital part of our world and its economy. The Carrier Corporation is one of the leaders in the industry, reporting employment of more than 45,000 individuals and sales of $15 million in 2007. According to Fueloyal, a fleet and fuel management company, the top 2019 HVAC Companies in the U.S. are, in descending order, Seimens Building Technologies, Goodman, Rheem, Trane, Inc., Lennox International, Johnson Control, and Daiken Industries.

Had Dr. Gorrie been born 50 years later, things certainly may have ended differently for him and his descendants. After all, five decades made a vast difference in technological capability. This time difference would have left Dr. Gorrie to be recognized in an entirely different light. Dr. Gorrie was "ahead of his time," and accurate recognition and appreciation for his work would not come until many years after he died.

Many of today's HVAC textbooks cite Willis Carrier exclusively for the invention of modern air conditioning without mention of Dr. Gorrie or his pioneering work. It is not known who or what is behind this omission. At this time, the Carrier Corporation website does not mention Dr. Gorrie at all. Of course, when a company can say, "the founder of our company invented modern air conditioning," that's a powerful marketing tool, and using this statement was likely an essential reason for his company's success.

Dr. John Gorrie had many admirable aspirations. He was highly intelligent; he possessed many other exceptional qualities as well. If John Gorrie had lived in more modern times, perhaps his invention of the ice machine would have been more readily accepted; his mechanism for air conditioning would have been easily recognized for its merit. If Gorrie he had lived longer, he may have been able to see his dreams unfold and receive the respect he so much desired and deserved. The world was not always appreciative of Dr. Gorrie, but, in the end, his work benefited mankind in ways he probably never imagined. In 1957, the John Gorrie State Park Museum was dedicated to his honor.

Although Gorrie was unsuccessful in achieving his dream of creating the large-scale production of artificial ice, much of modern refrigeration, air conditioning, and ice production is primarily based upon the fundamental principles he had discovered. As all modern air conditioning and refrigeration is dependent on air compressors, Dr. Gorrie's work in the fields of refrigeration and air conditioning are worthy of enduring recognition.

CHAPTER 12

Dr. Gorrie's Legacy and Pioneering Spirit Live On

INDIVIDUALS WHO MAKE important contributions to our world through their inventions, discoveries, leadership, and more are remembered, in part, due to the efforts of their descendants. As an example, Martin Luther King Jr., will always be remembered, thanks to the efforts of his descendants who carry his legacy forward. A federal holiday recognizes his fight for civil rights. Dr. Gorrie, however, had few descendants. For this reason, many people, even Floridians, have no knowledge of Dr. Gorrie.

In 1878, Dr. A. W. Chapman and Dr. Asa Gray walked on the outskirts of Apalachicola in 1878, 25 years after Dr. Gorrie's death. Dr. Chapman stopped and pointed to Dr. Gorrie's headstone, saying, "There is the grave of the man whom we recognize as the superior of us all."

In addition to the recognition Dr. Gorrie received during his lifetime, the following honors and events recognize Dr. Gorrie:

- The New Orleans Medical and Surgical Journal printing a summary of Dr. Gorrie's writings on the subject of fevers in 1853, the same year Gorrie passed.

- Dr. Gorrie's statue placing in the U.S. Capitol Statuary Hall in 1914 as a national tribute to him. Florida Senator George W. Dayton presented the statue. Florida Senator Nathan P. Bryan presided over the ceremony with The Southern Ice Exchange playing a part as well. Dr. Gorrie's great-granddaughter, Mary Louise Stewart, unveiled the statue, which was produced by Floridian artist C. Adrian Pillars. According to the U.S. architect of the Capitol, a New York congressman complained that there were "no great men" in Florida. In response, he received approval to construct Gorrie's statue.

• The Smithsonian's Natural Science Museum in Washington, D.C., giving full credit to Dr. Gorrie as being the father of air conditioning and refrigeration. The museum houses Dr. Gorrie's first ice machine as well as supporting patent materials. At this time, Dr. Gorrie's original ice machine is in storage. Officials within the Florida State Park Service are making an effort to return Dr. Gorrie's original ice machine to the Gorrie Museum in Apalachicola.

• On June 27, 1935, David Sholtz, Governor of Florida, issuing a proclamation designating the week of August 11–17 to be known as Dr. John Gorrie Memorial Week.

• The city of Apalachicola donating the land for Gorrie Square, located in the heart of Apalachicola. Gorrie's gravesite, the John Gorrie State Park Museum, the Apalachicola Municipal Library, and a memorial monument (donated by the Southern Ice Association in 1899) complete the square.

• The Liberty Ship SS John Gorrie navigating the Atlantic, Indian, and Pacific oceans on 21 voyages during and after World War II, before joining the Nations' Defense Reserve Fleet in grain storage in Oregon in 1957. The ship was built in Jacksonville, Florida, a product of the Saint John's River Ship Building Company. It was first launched on March 28, 1943.

• The citizens of Apalachicola naming Gorrie Bridge in 1935. The bridge spans 6.25 miles, connecting the east and west sides of Apalachicola Bay. The project took 18 months and $1,300,000 to build. It is one of Florida's longest bridges.

- Dr. Gorrie being officially recognized by the architect of the Capitol as the "Father of Air Conditioning and Mechanical Refrigeration" in 1938 when he engraved that very line on his statue.

- The Florida State University College of Medicine commissioning an artist to produce mosaic artwork images of John Gorrie, Elizabeth Blackwell, and Hippocrates—all noted historical figures in medicine. These images grace the entrance to the FSU College of Medicine.

Photo credit: Dr. Robert Watson

- The University of Florida College of Medicine presenting the John Gorrie Award each year at graduation. The award recognizes the graduating senior who "shows the best promise of becoming a physician of the highest type" and is based on grade point average, licensing exam scores, service, character, leadership, professionalism, and humanism. A crystal trophy and Vivian Sherlock's biography on Dr. Gorrie entitled *The Fever Man* accompany the award. Future recipients will receive a copy of this biography instead of Sherlock's. Following are the most recent recipients of this award (note that in both 2011 and 2017, there was a "tie" and two graduates were recognized):

  - 2008—Eric Ritchie, MD

  - 2009—Deirdre Pachman, MD

  - 2010—Farokh Demehri, MD

  - 2012—Christa Matrone, MD

  - 2013—Jennifer Goetz, MD

  - 2014—James Medley, MD

  - 2015—Lauren Page Black, MD

  - 2016—Samuel Lipten, MD

  - 2017—Jonathan Berry, MD and Matthew Huber, MD

  - 2018—Douglas Bennion, Ph.D.

  - 2019—Leora Leiberman, MD

Award made by Frabel Award Company. Photo credit: Leora Leiberman, MD

Leora Leiberman receiving the John Gorrie Award. Photo credit: UF College of Medicine

- In 1897, The Southern Ice Association presenting a plan that resulted in the erection of a monument to Dr. Gorrie's memory. A committee, chaired by a Captain Whiteside, commissioned the monument, which was erected in 1899. The monument, located in Gorrie Square, is quite impressive. The top of the memorial features a large urn draped with a veil, representative of a method by which tropical diseases could, supposedly, be prevented. Each of the four sides of the monument bears an inscription:

  - "Dr. John Gorrie, born in Charleston, SC, October 3, 1802 [sic]. Died at Apalachicola June 16, 1855. Inventor of the ice machine and refrigeration as described in his patent, No. 8,080, August 22, 1850. A pioneer who devoted his talents to the benefit of mankind. This monument was erected by the Southern Ice Exchange, 1899."

- The memorial at Gorrie Square being dedicated on April 30, 1900. Although Captain Whiteside was not in attendance, Judge George P. Raney presided, saying the following in closing:

  Never has [a] physician lived and commanded among his neighbors greater confidence than did Dr. Gorrie … His loving neighbors have been the adorers of his character and the perpetuators of his fame as a physician and a man.

- John Gorrie Jr. High School in Jacksonville, Florida being built in 1923. Although it closed in 1997, the school was restored and repurposed into The John Gorrie, A Condominium about a decade later. Jacksonville resident Delores Barr Weaver was the genius behind this effort. Classrooms were converted to residences. Great effort was made to retain much of the original features of the school. For example, near the entrance, one will find some of the seats that were part of the auditorium. The teacher's mailboxes grace a nearby hallway. School yearbooks, teaching supplies, and many photographs serve as a remembrance that John Gorrie Condominiums were once a place of learning.

An early image of John Gorrie Jr. High School.

An image of The John Gorrie condominiums.

- On August 16, 2014, the citizens of Apalachicola and Franklin County celebrating Dr. Gorrie's accomplishments with a "Festival of Ice," also known as "John Gorrie Day." This day celebrates Dr. Gorrie's contribution to our lives. The event features an ice carving competition, snow cones, and ice cream—all of which had been made possible by Dr. Gorrie's accomplishments.

- Dr. Gorrie becoming part of the Florida Inventor's Hall of Fame in 2014. On this occasion, which coincided with that year's "Festival of Ice," Apalachicola Mayor Van W. Johnson Sr., proclaimed, "[We] express our humble appreciation to Dr. John Gorrie and further dedicate the annual 2014 Water Street 'Festival of Ice' in his honor to coincide with his induction in the Florida Inventors Hall of Fame."

- The John Gorrie State Park Museum receiving approximately 8,000 visitors each year.

The museum opened in 1957 and is located at 46 Sixth St., Apalachicola, Florida. The historical marker reads as follows:

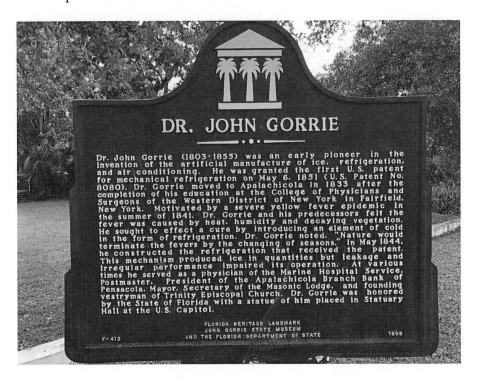

DR. JOHN GORRIE

Dr. John Gorrie (1803-1855) was an early pioneer in the invention of the artificial manufacture of ice, refrigeration, and air conditioning. He was granted the first U.S. patent for mechanical refrigeration on May 6, 1851 (U.S. Patent No. 8080). Dr. Gorrie moved to Apalachicola in 1833 after the completion of his education at the College of Physicians and Surgeons of the Western District of New York in Fairfield, New York. Motivated by a severe yellow fever epidemic in the summer of 1841, Dr. Gorrie and his predecessors felt the fever was caused by heat, humidity and decaying vegetation. He sought to effect a cure by introducing an element of cold in the form of refrigeration. Dr. Gorrie noted, "Nature would terminate the fevers by the changing of seasons." In May 1844, he constructed the refrigeration that received the patent. This mechanism produced ice in quantities but leakage and irregular performance impaired its operation. At various times he served as a physician of the Marine Hospital Service, Postmaster, President of the Apalachicola Branch Bank of Pensacola, Mayor, Secretary of the Masonic Lodge, and founding vestryman of Trinity Episcopal Church. Dr. Gorrie was honored by the State of Florida with a statue of him placed in Statuary Hall at the U.S. Capitol.

FLORIDA HERITAGE LANDMARK
JOHN GORRIE STATE MUSEUM
F-413   AND THE FLORIDA DEPARTMENT OF STATE   1899

- The city of Tampa, Florida, and the Hillsborough County District Schools taking great pride in John B. Gorrie Elementary School. This historic and lovely school is the oldest operating elementary school in the state and has an enduring reputation of offering outstanding educational opportunities to students in the Hyde Park Community. Gorrie Elementary has been recognized as a National School of Excellence.

At John B. Gorrie Elementary School, Dr. Gorrie's legacy and accomplishments are remembered and respected. The administration, faculty, staff, and students proudly celebrated the school's 125th anniversary in 2015. Many renovations have taken place, allowing the school to serve three generations of students. An energetic and very active PTA supports the faculty, staff, and students.

- In 1935, the John Gorrie Memorial Foundation was incorporated in Florida. Although it is no longer in existence, it was developed to "perpetuate the memory of the Florida physician, who, in his efforts to relieve suffering humanity and without a penny of reward, conceived and first applied the principles of refrigeration and artificial ice-making as we now know them."

- The John Gorrie Dog Park, located in the historic community of Riverside, in Jacksonville, FL, being opened September 17, 2016. It is located at 2623 Herschel Street.

It is also interesting to note that, in 1881, a version of Dr. Gorrie's cooling system (i.e., air flowing over cold, wet cloths) was used on the 20th U.S. president following his assassination attempt. President James Garfield suffered from a severe infection after being struck by a bullet. Garfield lingered for several weeks after the shooting but eventually died from the infection.

Modern refrigeration and the availability of artificial ice have changed the way we live. Much of modern refrigeration and ice production is still based upon the principles of thermodynamics studied by Dr. Gorrie. The availability of ice, no matter what the season, helped to transform Florida and the nation as a whole.

Truly, artificial ice, and Dr. Gorrie, changed the world!

Timeline of Dr. Gorrie's Life

1803
Dr. Gorrie born in Charlestown, Nevis on October 3

1804–1805
Dr. Gorrie travels to Charleston, South Carolina, with Mother

1805
Frederick Tudor (an "ice king") begins harvesting ice for sale/distribution

1825–1827
Dr. Gorrie attends medical school in New York

1827–1830
Dr. Gorrie practices medicine in Charleston, South Carolina

1830
Dr. Gorrie's mother dies

1833
Dr. Gorrie opens a medical practice in Apalachicola, Florida

1835
Dr. Gorrie appointed as an Apalachicola city council member

1836
Dr. Gorrie becomes president of the Bank of Pensacola, Apalachicola branch

Dr. Gorrie appointed vice mayor of Apalachicola

1837–1844
Dr. Gorrie serves as resident physician of the Marine Hospital Services

1837
Dr. Gorrie and others found the Trinity Episcopal Church

Dr. Gorrie becomes founding member of the Marine Insurance Bank of Apalachicola

Dr. Gorrie elected mayor of Apalachicola

1838
Dr. Gorrie marries Caroline Beaman

1841
Dr. Gorrie appointed Franklin County's justice of the peace

1845
Florida becomes a state

1849
Dr. Gorrie's ice machine (manufactured by Cincinnati Iron Works) is publicly demonstrated for the first time

1855
Dr. John Gorrie dies

1868
The first commercial ice factory opens in New Orleans, Louisiana

Dr. Gorrie patents the first machine that made artificial ice

The New Orleans Medical and Surgical Journal publishes a summary of Dr. Gorrie's writing on fevers

1881
Physicians attempted to save President James Garfield's life following an assassination attempt by using Dr. Gorrie's methods for cooling the air.

1902
Inventor Willis Carrier invents and presents an electrical air conditioning unit to the public

1914
Dr. Gorrie's statue placed in the U.S. Capitol Statuary Hall

1982
The first biography of Dr. Gorrie (*The Fever Man*) published

A Tribute to Others

MANY TYPES OF health professionals assist today's physicians by maintaining patient records, taking vitals, and facilitating communication between the medical staff and patient. Health professionals also assist with proper management of an office or healthcare facility. Many regulations and professional standards must be met to provide medical services to patients. In Dr. Gorrie's day, however, it was not common for physicians to have the assistance of others; they often worked alone. Additionally, although professionally trained physicians were licensed, there was no licensure for anyone who assisted physicians as they worked. Today, all professionals that assist physicians in the implementation of patient care receive some college training and are licensed through the state where they work.

In terms of the various professionals that work within it, the healthcare environment is quite complex during these more modern times. All health professionals that are not physicians are referred to, as a group, as "allied health professionals." This group of medical professionals would include nurses, pharmacists, medical assistants, physicians' assistants, physical therapists, certified nursing assistants, medical billers, etc. Because many people do not know the differences between nurses and medical assistants and the duties they perform, the individuals who serve in these capacities are referred to, collectively, as "nurses." There are distinct differences in their training and duties, however. Medical assistants only have about six to nine months of training whereas RNs and LPNs have much more training. Nurses also earn a higher salary than medical assistants.

Just as modern doctors, whose patient loads vary based on the health issues of the community they serve, Dr. Gorrie would carry a large patient load during the fever seasons. He couldn't have provided proper medical care to patients in three locations all by himself, so he relied on the support of two individuals, both mentioned in the 1982 biography, *The Fever Man*. His nurse was recognized, by title, as a nurse. Another individual who assisted Dr. Gorrie in his work was a slave named Gus. Although the assistance of both the nurse and Gus was crucial to Dr. Gorrie's success, there is little known about them. Regrettably, Dr. Gorrie's personal, patient, and professional records were accidentally destroyed, so we will never know, with any certainty, what assistance he had as he strove to care for patients in the best way possible. Although Gus was never formally given the title of medical assistant—as no one was prior to the 1950s—when his duties are contrasted to the duties of today's medical assistants, it can be recognized that he was a pioneer in his field. Gus was one of Florida's first medical assistants, and he would have gained much personal satisfaction from his work.

Dr. Gorrie's nurse would have provided any care measures that he ordered for patients. She would also have administered medications and made and recorded observations that would be useful to Dr. Gorrie as each patient's care progressed. Her job would have been to do everything she could do to keep the patient as comfortable as possible by providing the basic needs for each patient (clean bed/linen, food, and water). Although it was not the professional responsibility of his nurse to work with Dr. Gorrie's first cooling systems, she made an important observation one morning. When she discovered that ice had accumulated on the apparatus, she informed Dr. Gorrie; this was a big step that led to Dr. Gorrie's patent for the first mechanical ice-making system.

Despite being labeled as a slave, Gus' responsibilities would have been similar to the duties of medical assistants today. Gus assisted Dr. Gorrie's nurse when it came to any non-medical needs and would often venture into the swamps to find plant products that Dr. Gorrie needed for medicinal purposes—an unenviable errand. The swamps were ridden with snakes and alligators, so Gus is certainly worthy of respect. In addition, he would have been the person responsible for bringing general medical supplies, as well as food and water, to facilities groups. Disposal of human and medical waste would have also been Gus' responsibility. Because the goal of making artificial ice was considered, by Dr. Gorrie, to be critical for patient comfort, he may have assisted Dr. Gorrie as he built his first ice machine. Living in Dr. Gorrie's home and working so closely in the medical environment and with patients must have made many question Gus' status as a slave altogether and acknowledge his role in Gorrie's success.

Dr. Gorrie was respectful to all, and he was not the type to hold prejudice in his heart. This is the type of internal value that benefits all humanity, then, and, of course, today. It's another of the ways that Dr. Gorrie was "ahead of his time."

Afterword

Joshua Hodson
Manager of the John Gorrie Museum State Park

D R. GORRIE is the godfather, if you will, of modern refrigeration and air conditioning. A very ingenious person, Dr. Gorrie combined his talents and knowledge to be the first person to invent a machine that produced artificial ice. As a testament to his outstanding character and compassion, Dr. Gorrie frequently placed his own health at risk to treat yellow fever patients and save lives. He was also a respected servant to his community. He was a founding vestryman of Apalachicola's Trinity Episcopal Church and served as postmaster and mayor of Apalachicola.

Many have never heard of Dr. Gorrie or have even thought twice about how difficult life was before modern refrigeration and ice became readily available to almost everyone. Dr. Gorrie's ice machine paved the way for many significant modern conveniences. In Florida, especially, what would we do without modern refrigeration and ice? Refrigerated transportation allows for the distribution of foods to areas other than the location where they were grown or produced. Indeed, Dr. Gorrie's accomplishments are of tremendous value to our modern lifestyle.

The accolades for inventing modern air conditioning go to Willis Carrier. He founded the Carrier Corporation in June of 1915. It should be remembered, however, that it was Dr. Gorrie's research, methods, and principles that made Carrier's invention possible. Carrier's first modern air conditioner was introduced more than 50 years after Dr. Gorrie's death.

Each state in our nation is permitted to erect two statues in the U.S. Capitol Statuary Hall in Washington, D.C. If you visit our nation's capital, you will find a beautiful marble statue of Dr. Gorrie, representing Florida. In 2014, Dr. Gorrie was also recognized as one of Florida's "Inventors of the Year," earning him a spot in the Florida Inventor's Hall of Fame. His medal, along with other awards, is housed in the John Gorrie Museum State Park where the museum staff is happy to share Dr. Gorrie's story with visitors.

Each year, the College of Medicine at the University of Florida selects the graduating senior that shows the greatest potential of becoming a physician of the highest caliber. This graduate receives the prestigious John Gorrie Award. Other lasting legacies include a beautiful bridge in Apalachicola, an elementary school in Tampa and a Jr. High School in Jacksonville, Florida, that, now closed, has been restored and renamed as The John Gorrie, A Condominium.

If John Gorrie were alive today, there is no doubt that he would receive more recognition for his discoveries. Here, in the small coastal city of Apalachicola, on Florida's Forgotten Coast, we honor one of America's unsung heroes, Dr. John Gorrie. I take great pride in preserving his legacy and telling others about him. I am greatly honored to be the manager of the John Gorrie Museum State Park.

Joshua is a proud lifelong resident of Florida. He grew up in Islamorada and received his BS in geography, from Florida State University. Mr. Hodson has enjoyed an accomplished 18-year career with the Florida State Park Service caring for treasured areas and welcoming others to experience "The Real Florida." For the last 13 years, he has served as both the assistant park manager and park manager for three state parks: the John Gorrie Museum State Park, the Orman House Historic State Park, and St. George Island State Park. For five years before this, Mr. Hodson worked as a park ranger on Florida's east coast south of St. Augustine in the Florida Keys.

Glossary

Air compressor—a mechanical device that converts power into potential energy that is stored in pressurized air

Anatomy—a branch of biology that involves the study of an organism

Apothecary—an early name for a pharmacy

Blood meal—the blood taken in by a female mosquito when she bites

Botany—the branch of biology associated with plants and plant life

Brackish water—a mixture of both salt and fresh water

Communicable disease—a disease that is contagious and able to spread from one organism to another

Decaying vegetation—plant material that is no longer alive, rotting

Diagnose—the process of distinguishing one disease from another or determining the nature of a disease following a specific medical process

Dormant—a period of time when an organism's metabolism is inactive

Empiric—a person who, in medicine or other branches of science, relies solely on observation and experiment, not medical knowledge

Endemic—a disease that is prevalent in a particular geographical area

Epidemic—a disease that is spreading rapidly in a particular geographical area

Erythrocytes—red blood cells that are responsible for carrying oxygen (O_2) and carbon dioxide (CO_2) through the body

Fever—an abnormally elevated body temperature; one of the body's defenses against infection from bacteria, viruses, protozoans, and fungus

Health educator—a teacher or instructor that educates individuals or the public about healthy lifestyle and healthy behavioral decisions

Hippocratic Oath—a professional oath taken by all medical school graduates

Humanitarian—an individual dedicated to promoting the welfare of humanity

Humidity—the amount of moisture in the surrounding air

Hydrophytic plants—plants that have adapted to, and thrive in, low-oxygen (anaerobic) conditions typically caused by flooding or extended periods of saturation

Hypothesis—a possible answer or explanation for a question that can be tested by experimentation

Ice Kings—owners and operators of the Northern Ice Industry

Insect lifecycle—a pattern of four-stages that outlines an insect's life and reproduction habits

Insecticides—pesticides that are used to kill, harm, repel, or interfere with one or more insect species

John B. Gorrie Elementary School—the oldest operating elementary school in Florida, located in Tampa; formerly known as Hyde Park Elementary School

John Gorrie Jr. High School—a public school in Jacksonville, in operation from 1924–1997

Kinetic energy—the energy of motion

Latin—a language that originated in Ancient Rome, primarily used in science and medicine today

Leukocytes—white blood cells that are primarily involved in defense mechanisms that fight disease

Malaria—a communicable disease caused by a plasmodium; transmitted by the female anopheles mosquito

Medical jurisprudence—a branch of the law that relates to the practice of medicine

Medical *medica*—the body of collected knowledge regarding therapeutic properties of any substance used for healing

Mensuration—the science relating to measurement

Microorganism—organisms that are too small to be seen with the naked eye

Neuralgia—severe pain or discomfort along a nerve path

Nevis—a Caribbean island where John Gorrie was born (1803)

Oxygen—a colorless, odorless, gaseous chemical element that is necessary for combustion and metabolic life processes

Patent—an official document providing the exclusive right to produce and sell an invention or inventive process for a specified period of time

Pathogen—an organism capable of producing disease in another organism; a causative agent

Pharmacological—a branch of medicine concerned with the preparation, uses, and modes of action of drugs

Physics—a branch of science that relates to properties, changes, and interactions between matter and energy

Physiology—branch of science that deals with the events that take place during metabolism (of an organism)

Plasmodium—a mass of cellular material that contains no cell walls or membranes; the causative agent of malaria

Quack—an untrained person who practices medicine fraudulently

Quinine—a bitter alkaline in crystal form used, especially, for the treatment of malaria

Sanitation—the science and practice of maintaining hygienic conditions; proper drainage/disposal of fecal/urinary waste

Scientific method—an organized procedure that scientists use to answer questions, consisting of the following steps: stating the problem, forming a hypothesis, conducting an experiment, recording data and observations, and developing a conclusion

Stagnant—not moving, not flowing; foul from lack of movement

Survival rate—the expected percentage of disease victims that are expected to recover rather than die

Thermodynamics—a branch of physics concerning the relationship between heat and other forms of energy (such as mechanical, electrical, or chemical energy), and, by extension, the relationships between all forms of energy

Thermometer—a device used to measure temperature

Thesis—a research paper, especially one written by an individual seeking an advanced degree

Tonic—a drug or a medicine given to increase energy or health

Tropics—very warm areas of the world close or near to the Equator

U.S. CDC—the United States Centers for Disease Control

Vector—a means by which a disease-causing organism can be carried into a host cell, usually biological

Virus—non-living particles of genetic material surrounded by a protein coat; viruses use a host cell to replicate, or produce, more virus particles

Willis Carrier—(1876–1950) founder of the Carrier Engineering Corporation, recognized as the inventor of modern air conditioning

Yellow fever—a viral disease transmitted by mosquitos that has an incubation period and two stages in which patients will be symptomatic

Bibliography

"Achievements in Public Health, 1900-1999: Control of Infectious Diseases." U.S. Centers for Disease Control and Prevention Morbidity and Mortality Weekly Report (MMWR). July 30, 1999. 48(29); 621-629.

"Air Compressor." From *World of Invention* by Bridget Travers and Jeffrey Muhr qtd. in BookRags, Inc.

"Air Compressor." Wikipedia. Wikimedia Foundation, November 13, 2019.

"Carrier Centrifugal Refrigeration Compressor." Smithsonian National Museum of American History.

"Dr. John Gorrie." Canvas. https://canvas.instructure.com/courses/943080/pages/dr-john-gorrie.

"Empiric." Dictionary.com.

"Famous Floridians: Dr. John Gorrie." Exploring Florida: A Social Studies Resource for Students and Teachers produced by the Florida Center for Instructional Technology. 2002.

"France." History.com. https://www.history.com/topics/france.

"Gorrie Ice Machine, Patent Model." Smithsonian National Museum of American History, Behring Center.

"Historical Architecture Main Gallery." University of North Florida Digital Commons.

"History of Freemasonry." Masonic Service Association of North America.

"Inflation Calculator." CPI Inflation Calculator. https://www.officialdata. org/1850-dollars-in-2016.

"Intravenous Therapy." Wikipedia. Wikimedia Foundation, November 21, 2019.

"Inventors of the Refrigerator." FridgeFilters.com. 2018.

"Jay I. Kislak Foundation." Jay I. Kislak Foundation.

"John Gorrie: 1803–1855." Know Southern History.

"John Gorrie." Revolvy. https://www.revolvy.com/page/John-Gorrie.

"Laveran and the Discovery of the Malaria Parasite." U.S. Centers for Disease Control and Prevention. September 23, 2015.

"Life Expectancy by Age, 1850–2011." Infoplease. https://www.infoplease. com/us/mortality/life-expectancy-age-1850-2011.

"Life Expectancy." Wikipedia. Wikimedia Foundation, November 20, 2019.

"Mary McLeod Bethune." Wikipedia. Wikimedia Foundation, October 27, 2019.

"Photographs." Florida Memory State Library & Archives of Florida, Division of Library and Information Services. https://www.floridamemory. com/photographiccollection/.

"Smallpox." U.S. Centers for Disease Control and Prevention. July 12, 2017.

"The History of Medicine: 1800–1850." From the *International Wellness Directory* by Minnesota Wellness Publications, Inc. 2013.

"Thermodynamics." Wikipedia. Wikimedia Foundation, November 17, 2019.

"Transmission of Yellow Fever Virus." U.S. Centers for Disease Control and Prevention. January 15, 2019.

"Tropical Diseases." World Health Organization. 2019.

"Willis Carrier." Wikipedia. Wikimedia Foundation, November 5, 2019.

"Willis Haviland Carrier (1876–1950)." Smithsonian Institution Archives.

"Yellow Fever." Mayo Clinic. 2019.

"Yellow Fever." U.S. Centers for Disease Control and Prevention. September 12, 2019.

Aboukhadijeh, Feross. "1800-1825." Study Notes, LLC. 17 November, 2012.

Adrienne, Carole. "Medical Advances Timeline: 1800–1849." Civil War Rx (blog). 2015.

Alfred, Randy. "July 14, 1850: What a Cool Idea, Dr. Gorrie, Dr. Gorrie." WIRED. July 14, 2000.

American Mosquito Control Association. https://www.mosquito.org.

Architect of the Capitol. https://www.aoc.gov/.

Babington, Charles. "U.S. Capitol Statues Honor the Famous, Tragic and Odd." Albuquerque Journal. September 4, 2019.

Becker, Raymond B. 1972. *John Gorrie, MD, Father of Air Conditioning and Mechanical Refrigeration.* New York: Carlton Press.

Bells, Mary. "Nineteenth Century Inventions 1800–1850." Theinventors.org.

Berdichevsky, Norman. 2019. "The Florida Panhandle, John Gorrie and Air Conditioning." *The New English Review.*

BK-Hunters. "John Gorrie Junior High School - 1923 - Jacksonville, FL - Dated Architectural Structures Multifarious on Waymarking.com." Waymarking. November 19, 2015.

Call, James. "Rep. Ausley joins effort to remove Old Capitol Confederate memorial or add a treason plaque." *Tallahassee Democrat.* July 24, 2019.

Carrier.com.

Department of History, University of North Carolina, Charlotte. 1992. "Yellow fever epidemics and mortality in the United States, 1693-1905." *Soc Sci Med* 34 (8): 855–65.

Dhiraj Jindall. "On May 6, 1851 John Gorrie received a patent for an ice-making machine – This Day in Patent History." Patent Yogi.

Driscoll, Annelise. 2016. "The History of the Medical Thermometer." Withings (blog). October 18.

Dunn, Hal. "Dr. John Gorrie: the Father of Air Conditioning." YouTube Video, September 11, 2014. https://www.youtube.com/watch?v=_YgYn6ZlmoU&t=161s.

Florida State Parks. https://www.floridastateparks.org/.

Gladstone, John. 1998. "John Gorrie, The Visionary: The First Century of Air Conditioning." *ASHRAE Journal.* December.

Heimbuecher, Ruth. "THE 'REAL' FLORIDA STILL EXISTS, BUT YOU'VE GOT TO KNOW WHERE." *Chicago Tribune.* May 17, 1987.

Herchine, Thomas E., MD. "What is the mortality rate of malaria?" Medscape. April 26, 2019.

Hillsborough County Public Schools, Tampa, Florida. www.sdhc.k12.fl.us.

History.com Editors. "Civil War." History Channel. Updated September 19, 2019.

Images, Gado, Ian Dagnall, and Edwin R. Jackson. "How the Founding Fathers Understood U.S. Citizenship." The history behind U.S. birthright citizenship. National Geographic, November 1, 2018.

Kachur, Torah. "New study finds mosquitoes don't just lay eggs in standing water." CBC News. April 13, 2017.

Kennedy, John. 2016. "Florida's looking for help in replacing a Confederate." Post on Politics (blog). May 18, 2016.

Kesselheim, Alan S., Higgins, Susan, and Slattery, Britt E. 1995. *WOW! The Wonders of Wetlands: An Educator's Guide*. Maryland: Environmental Concern, Teacher Edition.

Leland Management. "Leland Management Welcomes The John Gorrie." Leland Management. January 2, 2014.

Lyons, Albert S. "The Nineteenth Century - The Beginnings of Modern Medicine (Part 2)." HealthGuidance. April 23, 2007.

Magoci, Jurica. "HVAC Companies In The USA: Find Out The 12 Leading." July 13, 2018.

McPherson, Laura. "The History of the Hippocratic Oath." Northeastern University Nursing. June 3, 2015.

Mier, Ruth Eugenie. "John Gorrie: Florida Pioneer and Harbinger of Air Conditioning." Master's thesis, Stetson University, Deland, Florida, 1938.

Morris, Allen C. *Florida Place Names: Alachua to Zolfo Springs*. Sarasota, Florida: Pineapple Press, Inc.

Morris, Elli and Wilkie, Curtis 2008. *Cooling the South: The Ice Block Era, 1875–1975*. Jackson: Wackophoto Publishers.

Morris, Elli. "Making Ice in Mississippi." Mississippi Historical Society.

Morse, Minna Scherlinder. "Chilly Reception." *Smithsonian Magazine*. July, 2002.

National Academy of Sciences. 2004. "Saving Lives, Buying Time: Economics of Malaria Drugs in an Age of Resistance." Ed. by Panosian C., Gelband H. National Academies Press. 5, A Brief History of Malaria.

Nelson, Josh. "Plumbing & HVAC Companies on the INC 5,000 List in 2016." Plumbing & HVAC SEO. 2016.

Rhoder, Henry E. 1854. *Dr. John Gorrie's Apparatus For the Artificial Production of Ice, In Tropical Climates.* New York: Maigne & Wood, Book and Job Printers.

Shah, Haleema. "The Unexpected History of the Air Conditioner." Smithsonian.com. June 24, 2019.

Sherlock, Vivian M. 1982. *The Fever Man: A Biography of John Gorrie.* Tallahassee: Medallion Press.

Spielman, Andrew and D'Antonio, Michael 2001. *Mosquito: A Story of Man's Deadliest Foe.* New York: Hyperion.

Taylor, H. Marshall. 1935. "John Gorrie—Physician, Scientist, Inventor," *Southern Medical Journal* 28 (12): 1075–1082.

The City of Tampa. "John B. Gorrie 125th Anniversary Celebration." YouTube Video, January 26, 2015. https://www.youtube.com/ watch?v=J_n8mttmyik.

The Editors of Encyclopaedia Britannica. "John Gorrie: American Physician." Encyclopædia Britannica. Encyclopædia Britannica, inc., September 29, 2019.

The Half Shell Channel. "Apalachicola Festival of Ice Tribute to Dr. John Gorrie." YouTube Video, July 22, 2011. https://www.youtube.com/ watch?v=PCmaMho9IFo.

Walker, Alissa. "We could have had AC 50 years earlier but the ice lobby killed it." October 22, 2014.

Wallenfeldt, Jeff. "Assassination of Abraham Lincoln." Encyclopædia Britannica. Encyclopædia Britannica, inc., April 30, 2019.

WhatsUpJacksonville.com. "The John Gorrie A Condominium Legacy Series." YouTube Video, April 29, 2014. https://www.youtube.com/ watch?v=dRJi0-hMasY.

Whitewaycorner. "The John Gorrie Dog Park." YouTube Video, September 19, 2016. https://www.youtube.com/watch?v=QgzgO9BOb-k.

Wildman, Don. "Ice Doctor's Invention." Video excerpt from *Mysteries at the Museum*. 2019. https://www.travelchannel.com/videos/ice-doctors-invention-0227058.

YourDictionary.com. 2019. LoveToKnow, Corp. https://biography.yourdictionary.com/john-gorrie

Zabriskie, George A. 1950. *John Gorrie, MD: Inventor of Artificial Refrigeration*. Ormand Beach, Florida: The Doldrums.

Acknowledgments

THE SUPPORT I have received throughout this project has amazed me. Many individuals have assisted me—far too many to mention. I will list those of most significance here.

This project began when one of my most memorable students, third-grader Santino Barrett, asked for help when he was seeking a book for a biographical book report. Santino enjoys science, so I suggested we look for a biography on Dr. Gorrie. It was then when I discovered Dr. Gorrie's last biography (*The Fever Man*), the one I read in 1982, was no longer in print. Upon learning this, I considered a new biography of this state hero to be of great importance; his legacy deserved it. If anyone deserved a new biography, it was Florida hero John Gorrie. I believe every Floridian should be able to find Dr. Gorrrie's biography in their local library. So, thank you very much, Santino, for coming to me. If you had not asked for assistance in finding a biography, I would not have known that Dr. Gorrie did not have a biography in print. I always assumed someone had written a new one and that, one day, I would read it.

The Florida Division of Recreation and Parks also helped me complete this book. Joshua Hodson, superintendent and park manager of the John Gorrie Museum State Park, assisted me many times by tirelessly answering questions, sharing information about the museum and state park, and reminding me of the value of preserving Dr. Gorrie's legacy. Several public officials in Apalachicola and Franklin County professed enthusiastic support for this project, especially Apalachicola's great mayor, the Honorable

Van W. Johnson. Officials at the U.S. Capitol Statuary Hall (offices of the Architect of the Capitol) supported me by providing information that I had been unable to locate.

Additionally, many medical and educational professionals provided assistance, proving to be of tremendous importance to me and Dr. Gorrie's new biography: Robert Watson, MD (Florida State University College of Medicine), Patrick Duff, MD (The University of Florida College of Medicine), Michael L. Good, MD (The University of Utah College of Medicine), and Mark V. Barrow, MD, of Gainesville, Florida. Thank you, also, to my good friend and University of Florida College of Medicine graduate, Shyam Paryani, MD, who stepped up when I needed to contact UF graduates who had received the John Gorrie Award.

Grateful appreciation is extended to the administrative staff of John B. Gorrie Elementary School and Principal Marjorie Sandler who allowed me to visit the beautiful Gorrie Elementary campus. Further gratitude is expressed to John Gorrie Jr. High School's media specialist, Mrs. Jean Powell, who provided tremendous encouragement as this project passed through multiple stages of development. My friendship with Jean has blessed my life in many ways

Dr. Gorrie's descendant, Ms. Jan Gorrie, was kind enough to review my publishing contract as well as the biography itself. Although I have only known her for a short time, it is easy to see that Jan emulates many of Dr. Gorrie's outstanding qualities. She is a person who cares about others, and her dedication to her family legacy is inspiring.

Thank you to my very talented illustrator, Karen Atkins, who worked diligently throughout this project and to respected Florida historian and author Toni Collins. As a published historical author, Toni offered valuable advice that I was happy to receive. Mary Merenda and Karen Kociemba of the Marion County Public Library System provided assistance that proved to be of great value as well. Mary secured a copy of *The Fever Man* despite it being nearly impossible to do so, and Karen helped me decide to pursue the project. She was quite enthusiastic. John Gorrie Jr. High alumni motivated me all along the way during this project. Of course, this acknowledgment statement would not be complete without expressing my profound appreciation to the author of *The Fever Man*, Vivian Sherlock. Ms. Sherlock's biography was a source of tremendous insight into many aspects of Dr. Gorrie's life that were not mentioned elsewhere.

Lastly, because admirable and significant goals cannot be accomplished without the love and support of family, I must admit that my husband, Gregory Caldwell, and daughter, Brittany Lin (Caldwell) Renkel played a big role in this project and my life. I love both of you very much.

About the Author

A LIFETIME FLORIDIAN AND identical twin, Linda Hansen Caldwell, was born in Jacksonville, Florida. As a child, she always loved science. She collected insects that she proudly shared with others, although some of her friends were a little squeamish.

Her father, Harold Hansen, taught her to play horseshoes, and she became a county champion. She also and spent a lot of time playing tennis and volleyball. When SEC volleyball was just beginning, Linda proudly wore #20 as a member of the very first Lady Gator volleyball team. As she matured, her stepfather, Robert Knorpp Jr. ("Bobby") became a very influential person in her life. He taught her to set goals and motivated her to work toward them. Linda admired him greatly and was always able to seek his advice when she needed it. Further, he always believed in her.

A combined interest in biological sciences, health, and physical fitness led her to pursue a career in education. Linda received a BS from the University of Florida's College of Health and Human Performance. As either a resource or classroom teacher, she taught many subjects in every grade from K–12. She taught health education and science at John Gorrie Jr. High School for seven years and later became a high school teacher. She also edited textbooks and curriculum manuals. Linda was recognized as a respected health educator in Duval County and was named as "One of Florida's Most Outstanding Secondary Science Teachers" when she was teaching high school science.

When Linda was 16 years old, she began collecting "button pins," with her collection approaching 5,000. Linda enjoys helping others and can have a difficult time saying "no" whenever and wherever her help is needed—be it at home assisting her family or donating blood at the local blood bank. Among her favorite activities, she most enjoys camping and spending time with her grandchildren. She lives in rural central Florida with her husband, Greg, and her basset hound, Barq's.

About the Illustrator

KAREN ATKINS has an AS in graphic design and has been a profes-sional artist specializing in watercolor since 1999. However, she also pursued a fine arts career. Today, she mostly paints watercolor portraits and architectural landscapes on commission.

She has created artwork for the Corporate Housing Expert's Buddy Bucks Program, and her design skills granted the program the award of "Most Creative Marketing for a Company with Less than 300 Units" at the National CHPA Conference and Awards Banquet 2013. Other recognitions Karen has received for her many talents include the Presidential Scholar Award in 1999. Karen was also recognized in the 1999 Collegiate Invitational, a top medalist in the Hood Boy Scout Patch Design Contest in 1999, a second place finalist in the 1999 Hinds CC Student Art Exhibition and State VICA Competition, and given an honorable mention in the 1999 MS CC Art Exhibition. Karen looks forward to expanding her painting career in the future. She resides in Seymour, Tennessee, with her husband William "Billy," her daughter Katelyn, her two dogs Nibbler and Kara, and her two cats Elsa and Flash.